Block bender Quilts

Margaret J. Miller

That Patchwork Place®

Credits

Editor-in-Chief • Barbara Weiland
Technical Editor • Kerry I. Hoffman
Managing Editor • Greg Sharp
Copy Editor • Liz McGehee
Proofreader • Leslie Phillips
Illustrator • Laurel Strand
Illustration Assistant • Lisa McKenney
Photographer • Brent Kane
Photography Assistant • Richard Lipshay
Design Director • Judy Petry
Text and Cover Designer • Cheryl Stevenson
Design Assistant • Claudia L'Heureux

Blockbender Quilts
© 1995 by Margaret J. Miller
That Patchwork Place, Inc., PO Box 118, Bothell, WA 98041-0118 USA

Printed in Hong Kong
00 99 98 97 96 95   6 5 4 3 2 1

Mission Statement

We are dedicated to providing quality products that encourage creativity and promote self-esteem in our customers and our employees.

We strive to make a difference in the lives we touch.

That Patchwork Place is an employee-owned, financially secure company.

Library of Congress Cataloging-in-Publication Data

Miller, Margaret J.,
    Blockbender quilts / Margaret J. Miller.
        p.   cm.
    ISBN 1-56477-107-5
    1. Patchwork. 2. Color in textile crafts. I. Title.
TT835.M519 1995
746.46—dc20   95-4634
                                                      CIP

Acknowledgments

My heartfelt thanks go to:

Mary Hales, owner of The Quilt Shop in Stanwood, Washington, for her unfailing good cheer and generosity to teachers and students of quiltmaking. The spirit of sharing, discovery, and support that she has nurtured in her shop over the past nine years is a great gift to all of us who make quilts west of the Cascades. It was in classes taught at The Quilt Shop that many of the quilts in this book were developed.

The quiltmakers, chosen from among my quilting friends and acquaintances whose work I admired and who accepted the challenge of developing Blockbender quilts in a three-class workshop, not knowing whether or not their work would eventually wind up in this book:

Janice Baehr, Avis Cadell, Nancy Lee Chong, Helen Gross, Vivian Heiner, Elizabeth Hendricks, Kerry Hoffman, Donna Holthusen, Marty Kutz, Dale MacEwan, Bonnie Mitchell, Mary Ann Musgrove, Carol Olsen, Reynola Pakusich, Betty Parks, Flo Peel, Doreen Rennschmid, Mary Ellen Rees, Julie Tollefson, Martha White, and Maggie Worline. These women, a number of whom have full-time "day jobs," devoted many hours, even during the Christmas holidays, working on the Blockbender quilt idea. They will never know how grateful I am for their generosity in time, enthusiasm, and devotion to this new project!

The quiltmakers from other classes over the years whose work was so generously shared for inclusion in this book: Valerie Sauban Chapla, Diane Lovitt, Marguerite McCallion, and Janet Steadman.

Maurine Noble, who despite being in the middle of preparing her own book on machine quilting, shared her precious time and magnificent expertise by quilting the cover quilt on this book.

My hostesses, as I traveled, who resisted the urge to treat me like a celebrity and a tourist and allowed me to sit quietly and work on this manuscript, especially Jean Wolfe of Marietta, Georgia, and Muriel Middleton of Ancaster, Ontario. Your warm hospitality and quiet support were most appreciated—as was Jean's at-home copy machine.

The employees at That Patchwork Place, who maintain their sense of humor as they manage to meet impossible deadlines. They produce many quality books in their quest to stay ahead of what quiltmakers of all skill levels want to know.

Dedication

To my sons:
David Andrew Miller, the sunshine in my life, who has always encouraged me to follow my dreams; and Allen Edward Miller, my special boy, who has taught me so much about life and love and persistence.

Contents

Preface

As we develop as quiltmakers, certain elementary truths become evident. For me, one of those is that the simplest patterns are often the most stunning and versatile. They can become vehicles for moving color and value across the pieced quilt surface.

Surely the simplest of patchwork shapes is the square. The repetition of this basic shape can lead to breathtaking quilt designs when you add value and color to the pieced surface. These range from the traditional Amish Trip Around the World quilts to those of contemporary quiltmaker Jan Myers-Newbury.

Another common shape in traditional quilt design is the triangle. In traditional patchwork patterns, the triangle most commonly takes the shape of a half-square or quarter-square triangle. As an equilateral triangle, it can be used as a basis for hexagonal designs. Traditionally, the triangle has been combined with squares, and less frequently with rectangles, to form our library of traditional quilt patterns.

Triangles, when used exclusively in pieced surface design, offer a world of design possibilities. This is especially true when two triangles form rectangles or squares. The magic of the resultant designs is that illusions are created when diagonal lines change from 45° to many other angles. The angled lines generate curves over the surface, even though only straight-line piecing is involved. In addition, when multiple-size rectangles and squares are used in the same design, the quilt surface seems to "bend" around columns, or pillars, or create other undulating patterns—hence the title, *Blockbender Quilts.*

In my study of color, I have found it helpful to assign numbers or letters to a range of color values and then apply those numbers to any given line design in an organized fashion. The wonder and excitement of this approach is that you can't be sure what the ultimate quilt will look like until the last piece is put in place on the design wall. Such an approach also takes the agony out of specific fabric or color decisions. Once all the pieces are in place on the design wall, you can fine-tune value choices if necessary.

Introduction

This book is not meant to be a book of rules or prescriptions for a limited range of quilts, and it is certainly not an encyclopedia of all of the possibilities for combining half-square and half-rectangle triangles. Rather, it is an idea book in which a few guidelines are given along with quilts that show how various quiltmakers interpret those guidelines. You are encouraged to follow your own "ripple in the pond" into which these design ideas have been dropped.

Blockbender quilt ideas appear as photos of actual quilts in this book, but many more ideas are in the form of line drawings and fabric mock-ups. Feel free to interpret these design suggestions in your own way, using them as jumping-off places for your own Blockbender quilts.

How to Use This Book

This book explores color and value strategies and line design. Throughout, discussion includes single-fabric triangles as well as strip-pieced triangles.

I encourage you to peruse the entire book before beginning any of the exercises, as the perspective gained from such an overview will help you develop your own design ideas more quickly. The Blockbender approach can be taken in many design directions. You will find it helpful to spend plenty of time working with the line designs and then with the mock-up format before committing to a full quilt.

The *Blockbender Quilts* system is first presented using single-fabric triangles and, later, strip-pieced triangles as the basis for design. The section on strip-pieced triangles builds on my book *Strips That Sizzle.* It is very helpful to have a copy of that book handy. Practice some of the basic exercises with Strips That Sizzle blocks before working with strip-pieced triangles for Blockbender quilts. The same strip-pieced strategies that were so stunning in Strips That Sizzle blocks "sing entirely new songs" when interpreted in the Blockbender triangles.

Keep an "idea book." Since the design potential for using half-square and half-rectangle triangles in combinations is vast,

you may find yourself getting ideas for quilts faster than you can process them! Keep a spiral-bound notebook handy for recording color ideas in the form of words, sketches, or quick charts. Use photocopies of the quilt grids found in Appendix A, beginning on page 130, as well. Ideas recorded in skeletal form in your notebook may be organized later in a three-ring binder. Your binder may also include pages with fabric swatches to record value choices for completed and future quilts.

Time is another important design consideration. Give yourself time to let the design evolve—observe your arrangements of triangles on the design wall at various times of the day and from different angles. Sometimes, when you come around the corner and see your design from a different angle, you may discover something new!

Remember, *speed* is not the goal; *delight in the adventure* of discovering new designs and new ways to sprinkle light over the pieced surface are your rewards for playing with Blockbender quilt strategies.

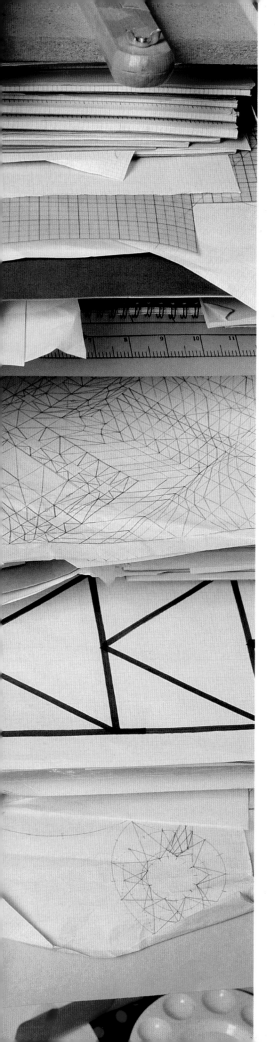

Designing on Paper

The first step in the creative process is designing and planning on paper. In addition to working with photocopies of the quilt grids (found in Appendix A), you should have the following tools and supplies:

Graph Paper Buy the kind that has 8 squares per inch with a heavier blue line printed every inch.

Tracing Paper You need a pad or roll large enough to cover the graph paper and quilt grids. Using tracing paper frees you to make mistakes, to record ideas as quickly as they come into your head, and to start over quickly when a design isn't going anywhere. You don't need to spend time erasing!

Rulers Try using two sizes of rulers, 2" x 18" and 1" x 6". I use the clear plastic rulers that have red 1/8" grid lines. Do not use your rotary-cutting rulers for designing on paper because the thick acrylic casts annoying shadows on the paper, making it difficult to draw lines.

Designing with Fabric

The fun really begins when you translate your designs into fabric. Of course, even though you have a design on paper, you may very well deviate from that design when you play with your fabrics.

The ability to choose fabrics and evaluate their success in your Blockbender quilt is aided by such tools as a color wheel, reducing devices, a mirror, and a camera.

I feel that the following tools are essential to good quilt design and color analysis.

Vertical Design Surface Stretch the fuzzy surfaces of flannel or Pellon® Fleece on a wall or cover a panel of Celotex (or soundboard). A design wall allows you to stand back and analyze your design as you progress.

Color Wheel Even an inexpensive color wheel can be an invaluable tool when you are choosing color combinations. Reference to the color wheel will be made from time to time throughout this book.

Reducing or Distancing Devices These tools that are the opposite of a magnifying glass, allow you to distance yourself from your work, making it easier to analyze your quilt's overall

color and design. A reducing glass is especially helpful if you have a very small space in which to work. Purchase a reducing glass in a quilt shop or office-supply store. Alternative tools include binoculars (look through the "wrong end"), the view finder of your camera, or a security peephole (the kind people install in their front doors).

Mirror Glaring design and color problems become immediately evident when you turn your back to the design wall and look at the design through a mirror.

Camera If you have a camera with flash capability, use it to photograph the layouts you discover. Later, analyze and compare the design variations. Snapshots of a quilt in progress often lead to many other quilt ideas—and thus a "working series" evolves.

Fabrics

Use good-quality, finely woven fabrics (those with a medium to high thread count). Cotton or cotton/polyester blends are best. Fabrics that are 100% polyester or those made from other fibers or weaves are not recommended, particularly in the strip-pieced triangles.

Color and Value

The theme of this book is "never use two fabrics when you can use twenty." When you use only three or four or even six fabrics to make a quilt, it may be obvious that one of those fabrics "doesn't quite go" with some of the others.

On the other hand, when you use many fabrics, the eye tends to blend all the fabrics together, and no single fabric stands out as a "misfit." For Blockbender quilts, you need to overcome the urge to agonize over every fabric choice; select many fabrics rather than fewer.

The value of a color is its lightness or darkness. The values of the color orange, for example, range from the palest of peach tones to apricot, orange, red-orange, red-brown, through the rusts, all the way to rusty loam and black-brown. Emerging quiltmakers find it a challenge to incorporate more values into their quilts—to go "all the way up through the lights" and "all the way down through the darks."

For many quiltmakers, it is difficult to buy light or light-medium fabrics. This is, in part, because many shops do not stock a wide range of light-value fabrics. Fabric manufacturers produce more medium to dark values than light and light-medium fabrics. Take a moment and look at all your fabrics. Does your collection have a good range of light, medium, and dark values? If not, on your next trip to a quilt shop, challenge yourself to buy only light fabrics if that is the value missing in your fabric collection.

When you are choosing fabrics by value, it is important to evaluate them from a distance. Arrange the fabrics so that approximately the same amount of each fabric is visible. Fan the fabrics in flat folds, arranging values from lightest to darkest. In a fabric store, stack bolts of fabric from lightest to darkest and then look at them from across the store.

Some people like to look at the stacked fabrics through a red or green piece of Plexiglas or a plastic report cover. I find it is just as easy to squint your eyes or view the fabrics in lowered light, such as late-afternoon natural light or in a room where most of the lights are turned off. As you squint, you see color less and value more.

To make your first Blockbender quilt, following the exercises in this book, you will choose six to eight values, ranging from very light to very dark, in each of two color families. During the selection process, try to find the same strength of values in each color family; that is, look to see that your darkest values are equally dark.

Do not agonize about this first set of fabrics. You will cut out *all* the triangles needed and get them up on your design wall, and *then* you will fine-tune your value choices. You cannot tell the final value of a fabric until you see it with the other triangles that are placed around it. What Jean Ray Laury said in a class on quilt design a few years ago applies here, too: selecting fabrics is a *visual* experience, not an *intellectual* one!

Later in the book, you will proceed from single-fabric triangles to strip-pieced ones. You will find that, when you cut the same fabrics that you used in the single-fabric triangles into strips and reassemble them, the fabrics may be assigned a slightly different value in your fabric lineup. This is not unexpected. If you cannot decide whether one fabric is darker or lighter than another, the two fabrics will probably be interchangeable. *Don't agonize—jump in and sew them together!* If your first group of fabrics included a printed fabric that could be placed in either color family, assign it to *one or the other*—do not use it in both color families.

Basic Line Designs

Blockbender quilts are based on the simplest of pattern shapes: squares and rectangles that have been divided into two triangles. In this chapter we will explore the amazing potential of these basic shapes and the single diagonal line that creates them.

To gain a better understanding of the Blockbender design system, make photocopies of the grids that appear in Appendix A and do the line-design exercises that follow. Make two copies of page 130 and multiple copies (at least a dozen) of pages 131–39.

In the first exercises, we will use copies of page 130. On that page, each traditional grid, consisting of all squares, has a corresponding Blockbender grid, which incorporates both squares and rectangles.

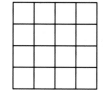 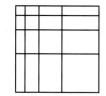

You will draw the same diagonal line to fill each corresponding interior unit of the traditional and Blockbender grids. In other words, the line design drawn in the traditional grid will be directly "translated" into the Blockbender grid. The diagonal line within a square will always be at a 45º angle to the sides of the square; however, when this same diagonal is placed within a rectangle, the angle will vary.

In the following exercises, consider how many ways diagonal lines can be used to fill the interior units of the traditional and the Blockbender grids.

One-Way Diagonals

The first line we will consider is a single diagonal going the same direction in every interior unit.

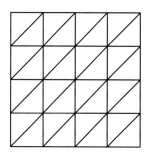 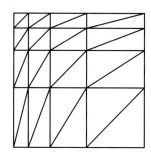

In the grids to the right, you see that changing the direction of the diagonal lines makes a big difference in the overall design of the Blockbender grid.

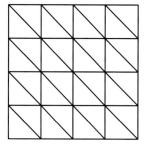 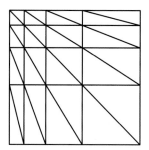

Two-Way Diagonals: Changing Direction Once

Place diagonals going two different directions in the same grid, alternating the direction once. Here the direction is changed down the center of the grid.

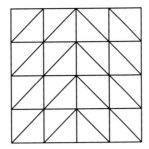 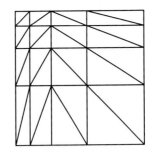

Here the direction is changed once, but not in the center of the grid.

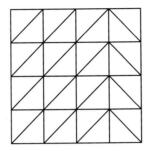 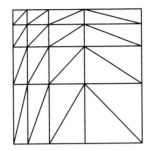

This pattern forms an "arrow" pointing in one direction. You can point it in any direction—north, south, east, or west.

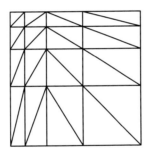 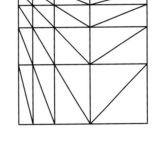

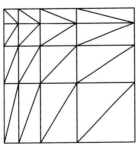 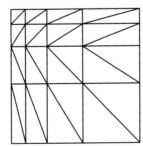

Parallel Zigzags

To create a zigzag design, alternate the direction of the diagonal line in the units for each row. In the example, the diagonal lines alternate horizontally in both grids.

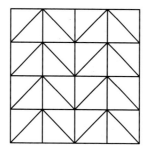 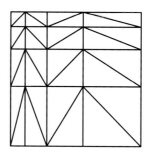

Experiment with drawing zigzags in a vertical direction as well. The difference between horizontal and vertical parallel zigzags is more pronounced in some grids than in others. The grids shown at right demonstrate obvious differences.

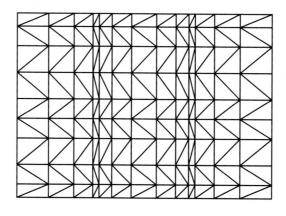

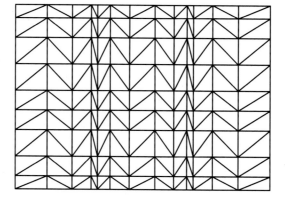

Opposing Zigzags

When you alternate the direction of the zigzags in each row, opposing zigzags result—and a network of diamonds appears!

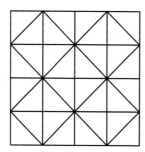 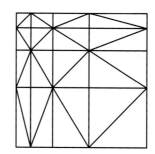

Enclosed Shapes

You can create a number of enclosed shapes on these grids. They can be either solid (created with a single line) or open in the center (drawn with a double line). Shown are examples of grids with solid and open diamonds. Other enclosed shapes include rectangles, hearts, a four-leaf clover, and pinwheel designs.

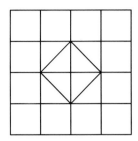
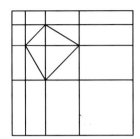
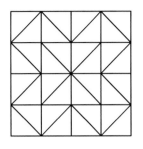
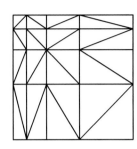

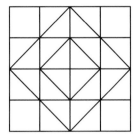
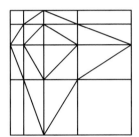
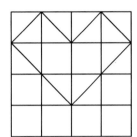
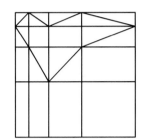

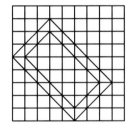
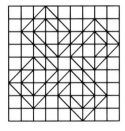

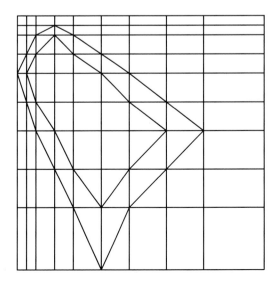
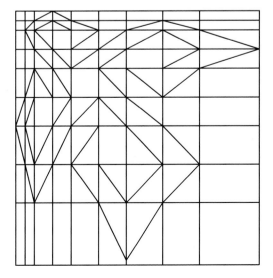

Radiating Designs

The opposite of an enclosed shape is a radiating shape, which leads the eye out toward the edges of the grid. The spaces around this X shape are filled with "echoing" lines.

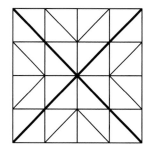
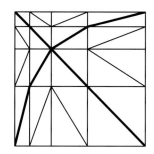

For the rest of the exercises, use your photocopies of Grids A through I. When you create a grid by combining narrowly spaced lines with widely spaced lines in both directions, a range of visual effects results. When diagonal lines are added to the grid units, an undulating, three-dimensional quilt design emerges.

Many more possibilities exist for grids than those provided in this book; I encourage you to develop your own grids. Draw perpendicular intersecting lines on 8-squares-per-inch graph paper. The numbers at the edge of the grids refer to how many ⅛" squares are contained in each unit.

Draw each of the line designs (one-way diagonals, parallel zig-zags, opposing zigzags, etc.) onto photocopies you made of grids A through I. This exercise will show you the tremendous design potential that exists in the Blockbender quilt system. For example, look at how different single-diagonal lines look on grids A, B, C, D, and H.

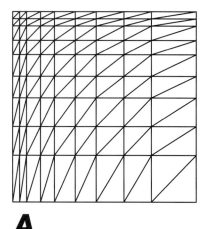

A

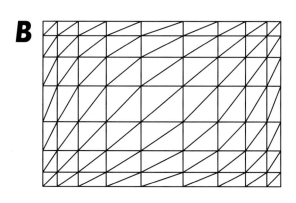

B

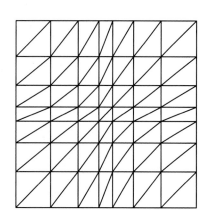

C

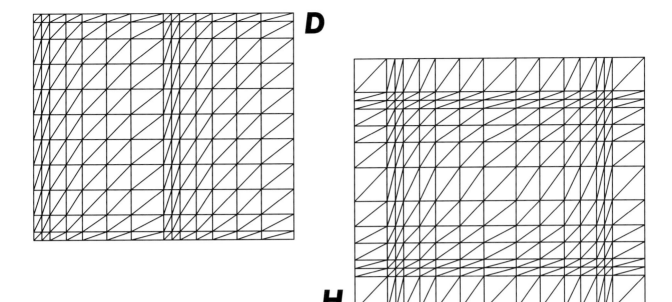

D

H

Random Zigzags

For the next exercise, choose a grid with many units (grids D through I). Orient rectangular grids horizontally rather than vertically. Begin at the left side and make a random zigzag line, creating what looks like a stock market chart. Now go back and add lines parallel to the original one. This yields a bargello-like pattern.

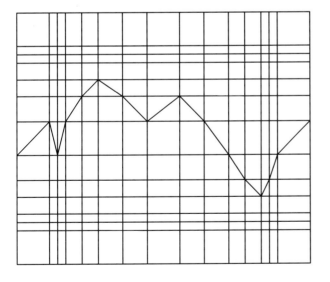

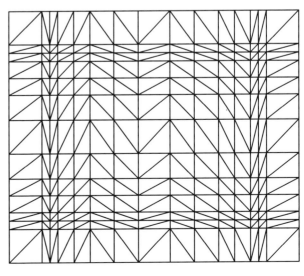

Random Shapes

The next exercise takes enclosed shapes a step farther. Using any of grids D through I, draw three enclosed patterns, choosing diamonds, hearts, or four-leaf clovers, in random places on the grid. One of the shapes may "fall off" the edge of the grid as shown on page 21.

Draw echoing lines around each shape until the three shapes "collide." Your challenge is to resolve the areas where the shapes merge.

Bonnie Mitchell, in her quilt "Diamonds," used this design approach, beginning with two diamond shapes and using Grid B.

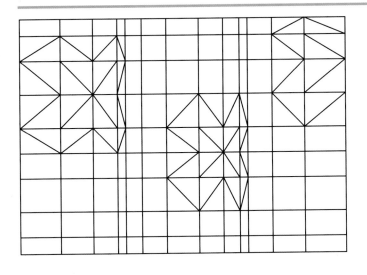

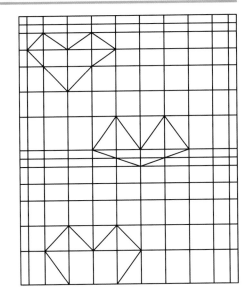

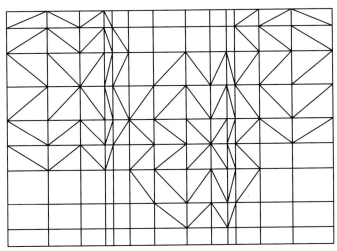

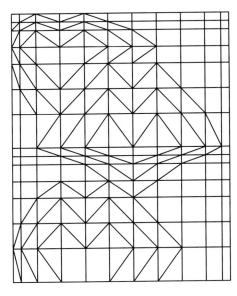

Echoing Shapes

Enclosed shapes can be used a number of ways on the grids. They may be used singly, with echoing lines that emanate outward to the edge of the quilt surface. Obviously, it makes a big difference where the "core" enclosed shape is located on the grid.

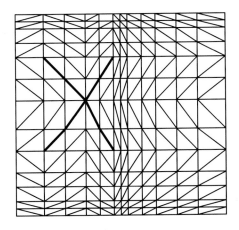

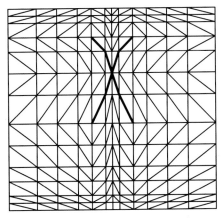

Overlapping and Interlocking Shapes

Multiples of shapes may be used other ways. They may be overlapped, giving the appearance that one shape is partially hidden by the other. Or, the area where the two shapes overlap may be used to mix colors and/or values for a transparent effect.

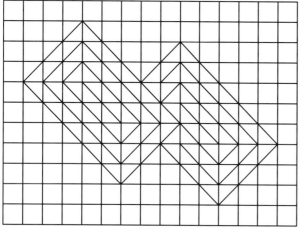

Overlapping

Transparent Effect

My quilt "All That Glitters" shows both kinds of overlapping. In the central band of motifs, lighter and darker diamonds overlap each other. Where the diamonds overlap, medium values were chosen to give the impression that you are looking through one diamond to the other one behind it. In the top row, the diamonds interlock; in the bottom row, each diamond is partially hidden by its neighbor to the left.

All That Glitters (detail) by Margaret J. Miller, 1994, Woodinville, Washington, 49" x 61". The full quilt is shown on page 48. ▶

When you use open, rather than solid, enclosed shapes, you can create interesting interlocking quilt designs. Open squares and rectangles are particularly versatile.

Elizabeth Hendricks used this design approach in her quilt "Chains" on page 46.

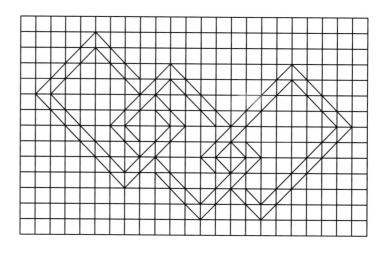

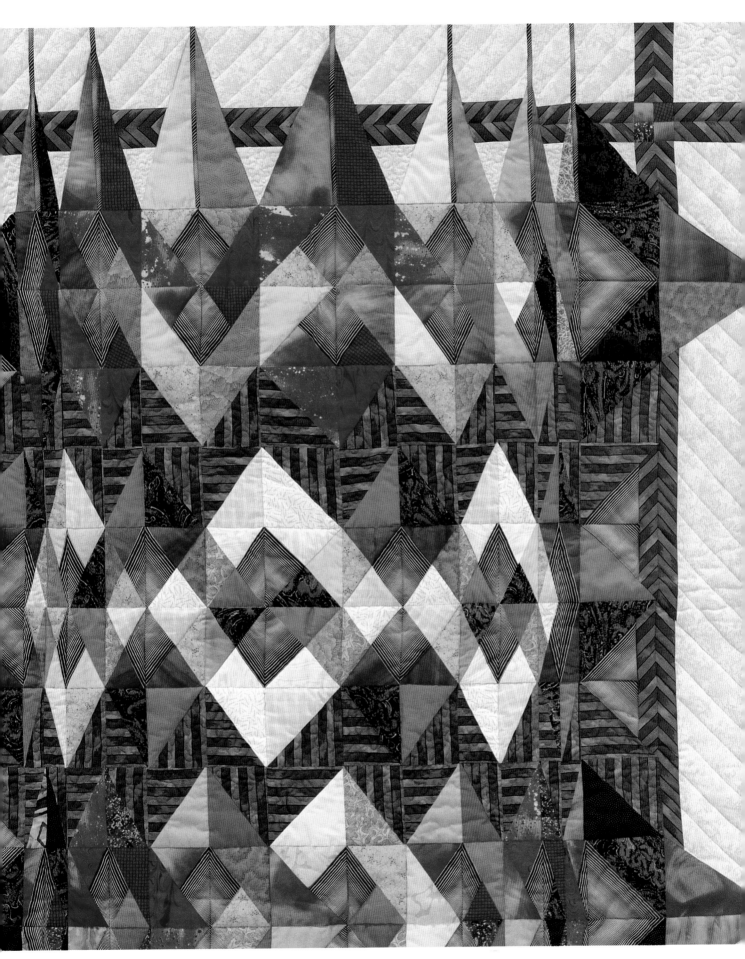

Shapes in Rows

Rows of certain shapes, such as diamonds and four-leaf clovers, produce interesting effects. In the case of the four-leaf clover motif, note what happens when the rows change direction in the quilt. Even when rows are oriented in the same direction, the shapes can be linked in different ways to form the rows.

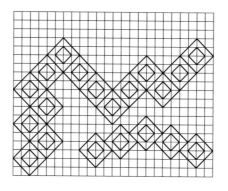

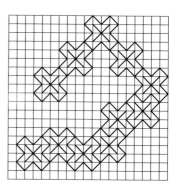

Chains of open diamonds are used in Avis Caddell's and Marguerite McCallion's quilt, "Pythagorean Pathways." By using two colors, they have achieved an interesting intertwining of red and blue chains.

Trail of Diamonds (detail) by Margaret J. Miller, 1994, Woodinville, Washington, 80" x 75". The full quilt is shown on page 49.

Offset Shapes

Making rows of offset shapes is yet another way to use enclosed shapes.

Offset diamonds were the beginning of my quilt "Trail of Diamonds," left. Note that the offset diamonds are a very small proportion of the total line design of this quilt. The background pattern and secondary ribbon motif will be discussed later in the chapter on strip-pieced triangles and borders.

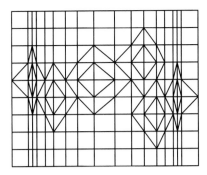

Split Shapes

Try splitting enclosed shapes and offsetting the parts from each other as in the heart example here.

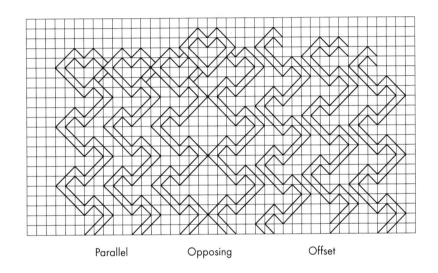

Parallel   Opposing   Offset

Pinwheels

The pinwheel is an example of a symmetrical shape that can be made asymmetrical. Explore what can happen when each arm of the pinwheel is a different length and the axis of the pinwheel is placed in different areas on the grid.

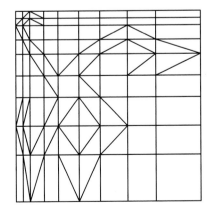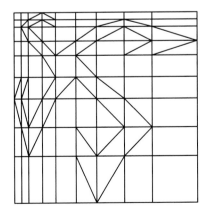

Asymmetrical Shapes

An asymmetrical shape, such as a heart, presents other design possibilities. Changing the direction of the shape in pairs or in groups can make a difference.

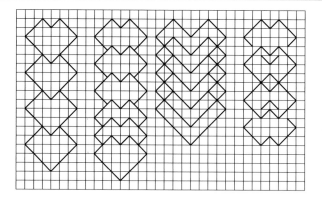

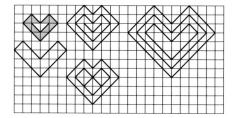

Notice the different corner treatments.

Julie Tollefson, in her quilt "Up and Down Blockbender Hearts I," used two identical heart designs assembled side by side in an inverted orientation. The soft flow of line from one heart to the other creates a special rhythm in this quilt.

A glorious example of what can be done with heart motifs is shown in the quilt "Turn It Any Way, We Love You," (on next page) designed by Nancy Chong and Elizabeth Hendricks. Note that there are two open heart motifs that interlock with each other: one is right side up; the other is positioned sideways on the quilt top. In addition, the hearts extend into the checkerboard border.

▲

Up and Down Blockbender Hearts I (detail) by Julie Tollefson, 1994, Camano Island, Washington, 46" x 35". The full quilt is shown on page 45.

Turn It Any Way, We Love You (detail) by Nancy Lee Chong and Elizabeth Hendricks and friends, 1994, Woodinville, Washington, 65" x 65". The full quilt is shown on page 49.

Random Diagonals

A very intuitive way of using the grids is to place diagonal lines (all going the same direction) randomly over one-third to one-half of the surface. Next, fill in any empty units with diagonals that go the opposite direction.

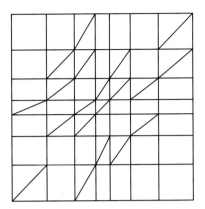
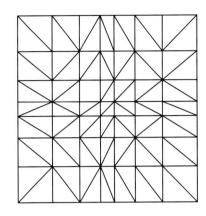

Combining Line Designs

The basic line designs explored previously can be used in combination as well. A quilt is always more interesting if the viewer cannot predict the pattern of the entire surface by looking at a small portion of it. A quilt that contains pattern changes from one area to another is more interesting to design and piece than one that has consistent design and color throughout. Study the examples where a combination of line designs appears on the same grid.

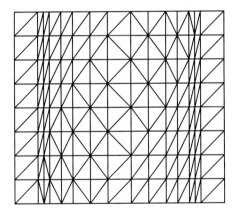
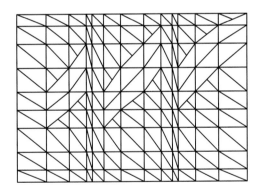
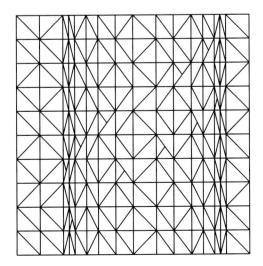
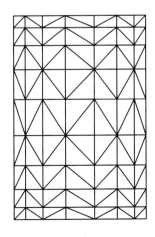

Try using the same line design in two different directions on the same grid. Orient them horizontally and vertically or along both diagonals within the same pieced surface.

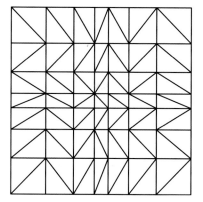

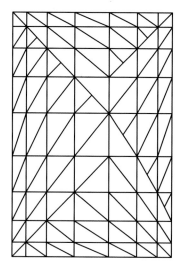

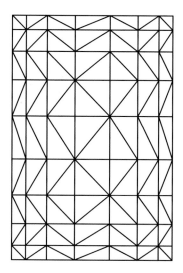

Helen Gross used this approach in her quilt "When I Am an Old Woman I Shall Wear Purple with a Red Hat II." Note that the bands of red go from corner to corner in both directions on this quilt. In addition, one set of red strip-pieced bands interrupts the other set.

If you choose an enclosed shape, you may want to highlight or set this shape apart from the background by using various background line designs. The first way is to draw diagonal lines all in one direction. Or, use the enclosed shape as a focal point and place echoing lines parallel to the edges of the shape. Repeat the echo lines until they reach the perimeter of the grid. An opposite approach is to use echoing diamond shapes that move toward the perimeter from the center of your enclosed shape.

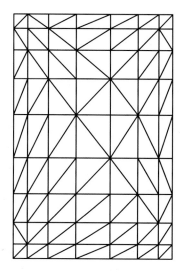

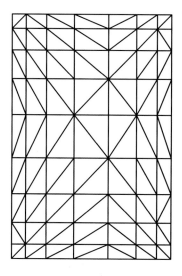

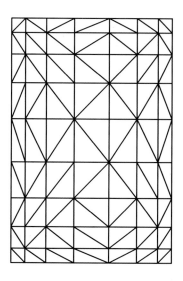

▲
When I Am an Old Woman, I Shall Wear Purple with a Red Hat II (detail) by Helen S.

Gross, 1994, Maple Valley, Washington, 52" x 52". The full quilt is shown on page 47.

Whether you use echoing or radiating lines, you have to decide where to place the center from which the lines emanate. Will it be the center of your enclosed design or some other point on the grid?

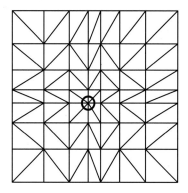

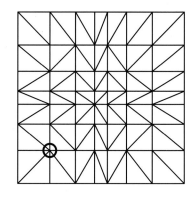

The open-diamond echoing design is very versatile for highlighting enclosed shapes. Again, the center of the diamond may coincide with the center of your enclosed shape, or it may be located elsewhere on the grid, independent of the enclosed shape it is setting off. Sometimes, to make a design look more complete or continuous, you may want to add a half-diagonal line within a grid unit. In the example, note that the background diamonds were formed with a combination of corner-to-corner and half-diagonal lines.

Around the Bend (detail) by Margaret J. Miller, 1989, San Marcos, California, 75" x 64". The full quilt is shown on page 47. ▶

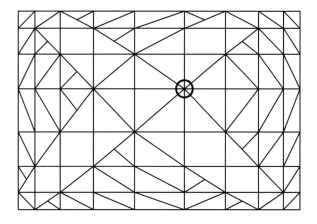

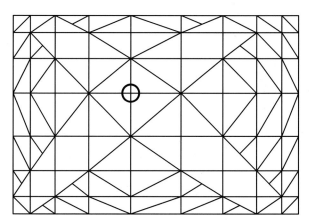

Ribbons and Bands of Color

Another useful line design to have in your repertoire is formed by parallel diagonal lines, which create ribbons, or bands, of color.

Use single ribbons or multiple ribbons. Repeat them, parallel to each other, or make the ribbons cross (intersect) each other.

"Weave" ribbons over and under each other to create yet another pattern.

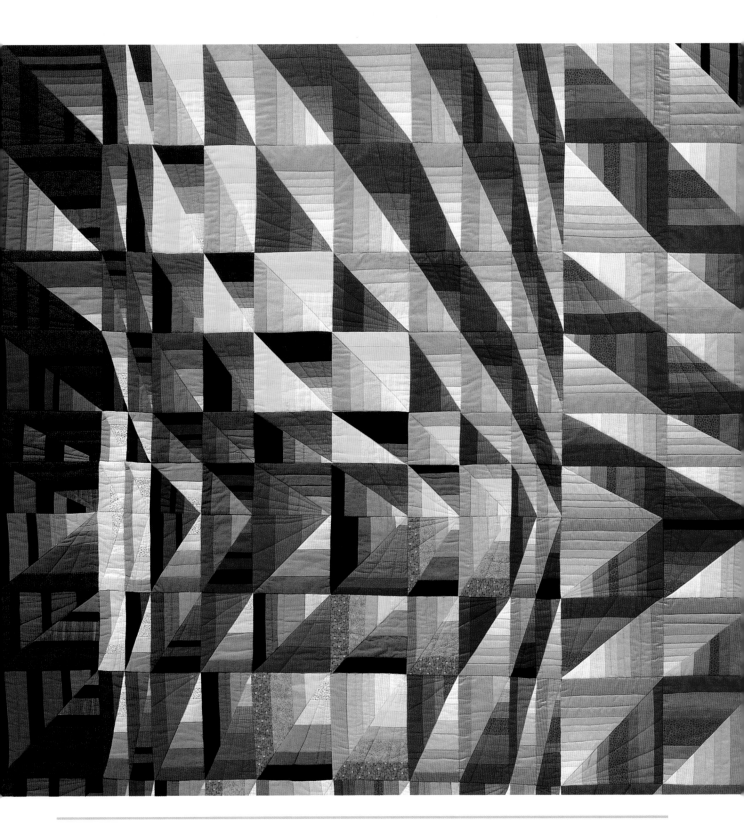

Parallel Bands

The line designs where all diagonal lines go one direction, or those where diagonals change direction once, are the most obvious examples of forming bands of color across a quilt. An example of the latter concept appears in my quilt "Around the Bend." Note that all the colors and/or values are aligned in predictable channels, except for the yellows. This approach brings a refreshing unpredictability to the overall color organization of this quilt.

Intersecting Ribbons

When bands of color are not parallel to each other throughout the quilt, they may intersect within the grid. Where bands intersect, you can choose to leave the square or rectangular unit "free of lines" or fill it with either a single diagonal or a double diagonal. Use an empty unit to blend the values and/or colors of the intersecting bands, thus creating the illusion of transparency.

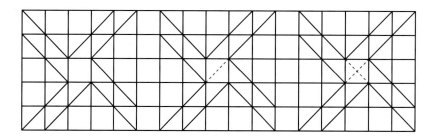

 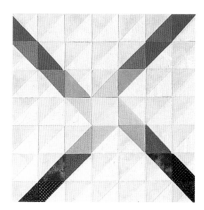 

When a grid is filled with double diagonal lines, a simple join is achieved.

A single diagonal line often creates an illusion that either the two bands are twisted around each other or they are "bent" bands adjacent to each other.

A slight variation of this design makes it look as though flat ribbons are intertwined.

   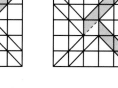

Weaving Ribbons

There are two ways to "weave" ribbons. First, the parallel lines that create the ribbon are not in adjacent squares.

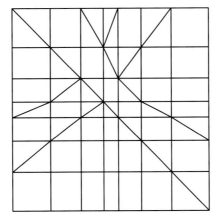

If you want a narrower ribbon, created by diagonal lines in adjacent squares, the crossing juncture is not formed by a continuous line, as it was in the previous example.

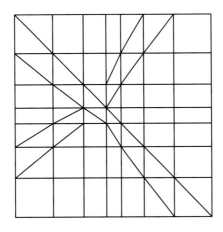

Intriguing designs in Block-bender quilts result from interweaving multiple ribbons, or bands of color, across the quilt surface.

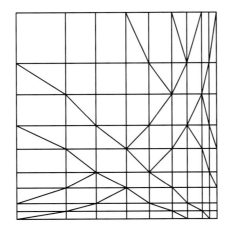
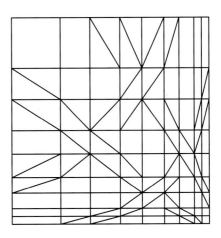

Half Diagonals in Weaving Ribbons

One way to make the weaving smoother when you are using narrow bands of color is to add half diagonals to the blocks, shown by the dotted lines in the illustration. To draw the proper angle for these half diagonals, be sure the line crosses each unit from corner to corner.

The bands of color could also be considerably wider than illustrated. In the mock-up, note that each ribbon of color is wide enough to accommodate six values that move from light to dark.

Mary Ann Musgrove, in her quilt "Running with Margaret," used the weaving technique to make strip-pieced swaths of fuchsia and green triangles meander across the quilt surface.

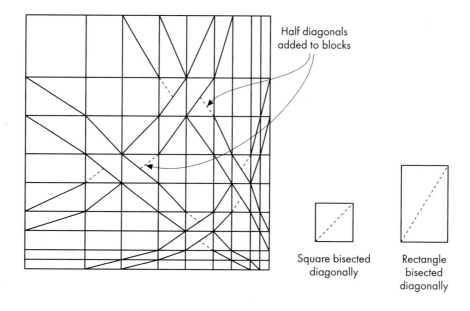

Half diagonals added to blocks

Square bisected diagonally

Rectangle bisected diagonally

◀ *The fabric mock-up (left) shows very wide bands of color and a patterned background formed by crossed diagonals in each unit.*

Running with Margaret (detail) by Mary Ann Musgrove, 1994, La Conner, Washington, 67" x 71". The full quilt is shown on page 46.

Folded Ribbons

Ribbons of color may also appear to "fold" in the quilt surface. This is where you can really play with lighter and darker values— to make it look as though you see the "right side" and the "wrong side" of the ribbon. The fold of the ribbon is created along a horizontal or vertical grid line. Two variations are shown here.

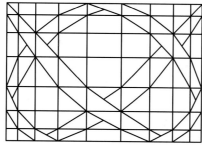

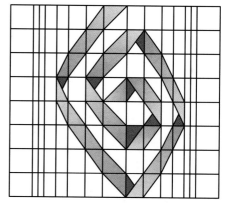

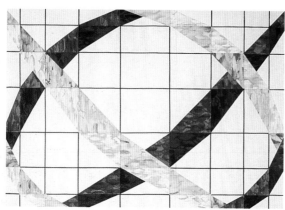

Experiment with narrow and wide ribbons in the same pieced surface design. Combining the graphic techniques of folding and weaving these "ribbons," or bands of color, can result in a very interesting quilt, considering the variation in the grids we are working with. In the mock-up on page 41, a single ribbon folds back on itself again and again to form a spiral. The ribbon changes from yellow/red to green part way across the quilt, and the green portion of the ribbon appears to spiral and weave over and under the red ribbon.

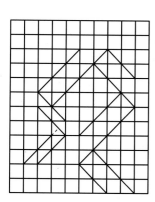

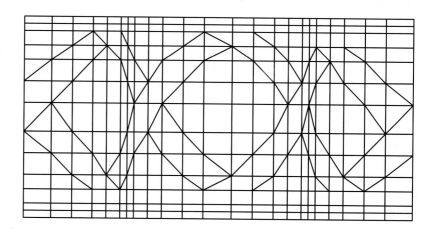

Developing Your Own Grids

Pick up the designs you did in the exercises on pages 18–22 and squint your eyes as you look at them. Note that designs in the closely spaced grid lines appear to be farther away from you. Conversely, designs in the widely spaced grid lines appear to be closer to you.

For example, hold Grid E (page 135) so it is oriented horizontally. It appears that a vertical column is in the center of the quilt; the two outermost vertical rows of blocks form a flat "ground" from which the column emerges. Grid I looks like a tufted comforter; Grid F looks like two billowing columns next to each other, with a narrow, deep space between them.

The spatial relationship is very important when you begin to apply color, to "sprinkle light" across these surfaces. To emphasize three-dimensional forms, try using lighter values where

the grid lines are widely spaced, and darker values where the grid lines are closer together.

I encourage you to develop grids of your own. To begin this process, choose one of the grids, A through I, in Appendix A on pages 130–139. Each of the numbers along the outer edges of the grid indicate the width of that unit, based on a grid of 8 squares per inch. For example, if the numbers are 4 x 8, that

means that the unit is four ⅛" squares wide by eight ⅛" squares long.

Transfer the vertical lines of the grid onto a piece of 8-squares-per-inch graph paper. Next, cover the graph paper with a piece of tracing paper. Below, the vertical lines from Grid A are shown. Draw horizontal lines on the tracing paper using a wide-narrow-wide spacing combination.

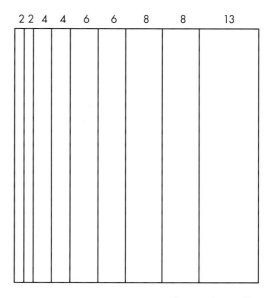

Replace your first piece of tracing paper with another, and try a different combination of wide and narrowly spaced lines. Refer to "Flights of Fancy" on page 114 for more ways to create your own grids. Later, in "Making a Blockbender Quilt," the grid system will be translated into quilt sizes.

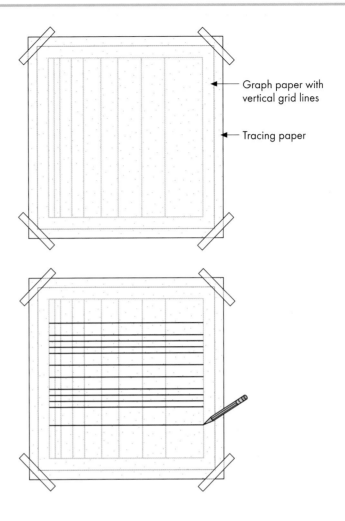

Graph paper with vertical grid lines

Tracing paper

Crossed Diagonals

Further complexity is possible when you fill each interior unit with two diagonal lines. I advise you to use this option with great caution and restraint, because the design area can be broken into tiny elements. Often, the results do not add significantly to the visual impact of the quilt. Explore crossed diagonals after you have played with designs involving one diagonal line in each unit. If you want to use crossed diagonals, consider using them as an accent only, or use half diagonals to complete crossing bands only when needed to strengthen the design.

In the mock-up on page 38, note how crossed diagonals form a textured background that accentuates the wide woven bands of value gradations.

Doreen Rennschmid used crossed diagonals in her pair of quilts, "Exploding Star #1" and "Exploding Star #2," on the facing page. She developed "Exploding Star #2" by using the leftover strips from "Star #1"! Notice what a different feeling each quilt generates.

Exploding Star #1 (left) and *Exploding Star #2* (below) by Doreen Rennschmid, 1992, Sardis, British Columbia, each 64" x 64". Exploding Star #2 was actually begun to break the boredom of sorting the leftover strips after making *Exploding Star #1*!

Crossed diagonals can also generate the effect of transparency. By crossing diagonals, you can create the illusion that one shape is beneath another and that you can see through the shape on top (the shape that is closest to you). In the area where the two shapes cross, you can mix color and/or value to produce the illusion of transparency.

By using crossed diagonals in my quilt "All that Glitters" on page 48, the illusion of transparency emerges in the middle row of diamonds.

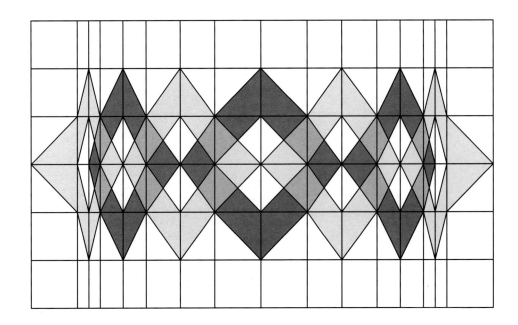

Diamonds by Bonnie Mitchell, 1994, Everett, Washington, 76" x 61". This strip-pieced Blockbender quilt features opposing light strategies: light in the center to dark at the outer edges in the background and dark to light in the diamond motif.

Up and Down Blockbender Hearts I by Julie Tollefson, 1994, Camano Island, Washington, 46" x 35". This was Julie's first attempt at a Blockbender quilt. She completed the heart on the left first but was unhappy with the quality of her piecing, so she hurriedly made the second pieced heart. When she brought both quilt tops to the second class, the joined "one up, one down" arrangement of hearts emerged!

Basic Line Designs – 45

Chains by Elizabeth Hendricks, 1993, Seattle, Washington, 80" x 60". Though the focus of this quilt is the interlocking open rectangles, note the subtle use of value in the strip-pieced background of this quilt.

Running with Margaret by Mary Ann Musgrove, 1994, La Conner, Washington, 67" x 71". Note the narrow ($\frac{1}{2}$"-wide) division between the quilt and its border, and the asymmetrical measurement of the border (6" wide on two sides, 4" wide on the other two sides).

Around the Bend by Margaret J. Miller, 1989, San Marcos, California, 75" x 64". Note that, in general, this quilt is bands of color that change direction in the middle of the quilt; however, notice how the yellow band is broken up so that the yellow triangles are not overpowering in this format.

When I Am an Old Woman, I Shall Wear Purple with a Red Hat II by Helen S. Gross, 1994, Maple Valley, Washington, 52" x 52". A good example of using the same line design (parallel diagonals) in two different directions. Note the phantom grid formed by the lightest values in the center of this quilt.

Pythagorean Pathways by Avis Caddell and Marguerite McCallion, 1994, Victoria, British Columbia, 59" x 38". This quilt using four color families (red, green, blue, and yellow) is an extended version of Grid H; it was extended according to the geometric rules for forming a Golden Rectangle.

All That Glitters by Margaret J. Miller, 1994, Woodinville, Washington, 49" x 61". This quilt shows various ways of combining enclosed shapes: interlocking the shapes (top row), using the illusion of transparency (center row), and overlapping the shapes (bottom row).

Turn It Any Way, We Love You by Nancy Lee Chong and Elizabeth Hendricks and friends, 1994, Woodinville, Washington, 65" x 65". Machine quilted by Maurine Noble, Seattle, Washington. This quilt contains contributions from all those students who were part of the experimental Blockbender class at The Quilt Shop in Stanwood, Washington. It was a gift to the astonished author at the final reunion of that class in May of 1994. Students were assigned various units of the quilt but were told only which *values* to use in their respective triangles, not which *colors*. Note how Nancy and Elizabeth carried the heart shape out into the checkerboard borders.

Trail of Diamonds by Margaret J. Miller, 1994, Woodinville, Washington, 80" x 75". This quilt features not only offset diamonds as the central motif but also a Blockbender interpretation of a Strips That Sizzle pattern for the background and an off-center "border within a border" in the form of a folded ribbon.

Color Strategies

It's All in the Numbers

Choosing colors for quilts is often a big stumbling block. There are many approaches to selecting fabrics for a given quilt, but the system presented here reduces the choices to a series of numbers.

These will, hopefully, provide you with a "jumping-off place" so that you are not paralyzed by having to make too many choices.

NOTE: This is not meant to be a magic formula for applying a range of values to quilts; it is meant to be used as a "start-up" system. After you select your fabrics, cut the triangles, and arrange them on your design wall, you can fine-tune your value and fabric choices.

Selecting Color Families

To begin, use a color wheel to select two color families. If you want your quilt to be quiet and subdued, choose two color families that are close to each other on the color wheel. If you want your quilt to be vibrant and snappy, choose two complementary colors, those opposite each other on the color wheel.

From your fabric collection, select all the fabrics that fall within those two color families and put them in two piles. There should be at least ten different fabrics in each pile. Next, arrange the fabrics, one color family at a time, in a horizontal row on a table, with the lighter values of the color on the left and the darker ones on the right. Arranging fabrics is easier when you squint and when you do this in a subdued light situation. *Don't agonize over this process! Just jump in and do it.*

Verifying the Complete Range of Values

Compare the two rows of fabrics. Have you gone all the way through the lights and all the way down through the darks in both color families? Do you have more medium values, with only a few lights and darks? Are your darkest values equal in strength, or do you have much darker values in one color family than in the other one? Make adjustments so that you have a relatively balanced range of light, medium, and dark values in both color families, with the same number of fabrics in each.

Making a Swatch Sheet

Cut a small (1" x 2") swatch of each of your fabrics and glue them by color family, from light to dark, in vertical rows on a piece of paper or a 5"-wide strip of poster board or cardboard. You will refer to your swatch sheet frequently, so it is important to make it portable between your design wall and work table.

Using a different-colored pencil (or pen) for each color family, number each swatch from 1 to 10, with 1 for the lightest value and 10 for the darkest.

These sample swatch sheets from various quilt projects can be a ready reference. Place fabrics side by side (with no white swatch sheet showing) to play with new color combinations.

Preparing Your Mock-up Fabrics

It is a good idea for you to illustrate each of the light strategies beginning on page 56 with squares of your own fabrics. This process will reveal the relative values you have selected. In a pieced surface, a single fabric is affected by the colors, values, and shapes around it.

Cut a 1" strip from each of your folded fabrics. Place several of the strips together side by side on your cutting surface. Tape the ends of the strips to the cutting surface as shown and cut as many 1" squares as you can. To keep your values sorted, draw grids of 3" squares on pieces of paper. Label each square with a number from 1 through 10. As you cut your 1" squares, place each fabric in the square that matches its value number.

To make your mock-up of each light strategy, use a glue stick to adhere your fabric squares to a sheet of graph paper. Apply the glue to the graph paper, not to the fabric.

Numerous squares can be cut at the same time for playing with mock-ups; cutting many squares before you begin makes the mock-up process much quicker and more enjoyable. ▶

Setting Your Attitude

Before you begin, remember that you are *not to agonize* about specific fabric choices; you are trying to determine how many basic ways you can *sprinkle light across the Blockbender pieced surface* and, eventually, any quilt surface. Learning to use color and value well in a quilt is a learning experience that is a never-ending journey—full of surprises. The more you play with color, the more you internalize a sense of how fabrics go together, and you become more skilled in the fabric-selection process.

For those who like signposts along the way, a good book on color theory will provide guidelines to speed you along. (See Bibliography on page 143.) Realize, however, that no single book or class will guarantee you instant success. As with anything, practice, practice, practice is what brings progress.

As you gain experience placing greater numbers of fabrics in the same pieced surface, you will realize that there are not just three categories of value (light, medium, and dark) but rather five: light, light-medium, medium, dark-medium, and dark. The day you pick up a piece of fabric and think of its relative value first before its color name, you will have reached a level of expertise well beyond the starting block.

Basic Light Strategies

Once you have chosen the complete range of values in two color families, the rest of your color decisions are based on how you want to "sprinkle" or move the values across the quilt surface.

Just as we explored Blockbender line designs by starting with the simplest line concepts, we will explore light strategies with simple grids and line designs.

As you focus on value placement, you will begin to appreciate the tremendous potential of these basic light strategies. Apply these strategies to your Blockbender quilt as well as to other quilts.

Each strategy in this chapter is first shown as a numbered open grid (no diagonal lines). The numbers indicate values from your swatch sheet. Remember, lower numbers represent lighter values (1 being the lightest), and higher numbers represent darker values (10 being the darkest). Alongside the numbered grid are fabric mock-ups of each strategy, first as a traditional grid and then as a Blockbender grid. These exercises are meant to show you how to think about sprinkling color and light over your own Blockbender grids of triangles.

There are many ways you can sprinkle light across the quilt's surface. The following strategies are not meant to be an encyclopedic review of such strategies, but rather, to be "jumping-off places" for you.

Horizontal Band of Light

Perhaps you want to create the appearance that a strip of light illuminates the top of your quilt. Therefore, the lightest values will be along the top row of blocks. As the eye moves toward the bottom edge of the quilt, the light becomes weaker, and thus the values are darker. The assigned value numbers begin with 1 in the top row (lightest value); the numbers increase in successive rows, down to the bottom of the quilt (darkest value).

In the mock-ups shown throughout this chapter, notice that, occasionally, two different fabrics denote a single value. This approach provides a better illusion of the light strategy than having an entire row of squares of the same fabric, as in the mock-up on this page.

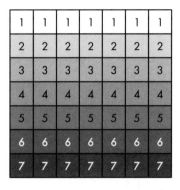

Vertical Shaft of Light

Imagine viewing your quilt from across a room, where only a sliver of light, coming through partially closed curtains, is cast on the quilt. To create the illusion of a vertical shaft of light, place your lightest values in a vertical row down the center of the quilt. The values darken (value numbers increase) as the eye travels to the sides of the quilt.

Diagonal Shaft of Light

Try placing the shaft of light so it falls from one corner to the other. In this case, arrange the lightest values diagonally across the quilt, and the darkest values in the opposite corners. In this color strategy, you use very little of your darkest fabrics.

When applying the diagonal light strategy to quilts made with triangles, it is often more effective to have a double row of the lights and multiples of the same darks in the corners to add strength to the color strategy. In my quilt "Gaslamp Quarter" on page 74, the same dark fabric is repeated in the last two rows of lower triangles on the right side of the quilt.

1	2	3	4	5	6	7
2	1	2	3	4	5	6
3	2	1	2	3	4	5
4	3	2	1	2	3	4
5	4	3	2	1	2	3
6	5	4	3	2	1	2
7	6	5	4	3	2	1

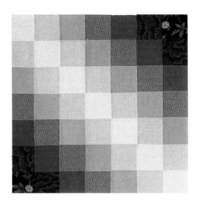

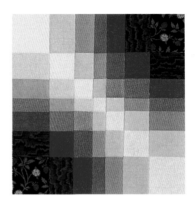

Spotlight Off One Corner

A variation on the "diagonal shaft of light" theme is to create the illusion that there is a floodlight shining on one corner of your quilt. In this case, place the lightest values in one corner, and the darkest ones in the opposite corner. Use more medium-range fabrics and fewer lights and darks.

1	1	2	3	4	5	6
1	2	3	4	5	6	7
2	3	4	5	6	7	8
3	4	5	6	7	8	9
4	5	6	7	8	9	10
5	6	7	8	9	10	10
6	7	8	9	10	10	10

1	1	2	2	3	3	4
1	2	2	3	3	4	4
2	2	3	3	4	4	5
2	3	3	4	4	5	5
3	3	4	4	5	5	6
3	4	4	5	5	6	6
4	4	5	5	6	6	7

One example of this light strategy in strip-pieced triangles is Marty Kutz's quilt "Lent." Marty diffused the light that shines from the corner, rather than using values as described in the previous example. Marty's quilt is a good example of how the light-strategy exercises presented in this section are meant to be used only as jumping-off places. Start with one of these strategies and, as the quilt develops, let the quilt tell you how strictly or loosely the strategy should be applied.

Spotlight in the Center

The illusion of a spotlight hitting the center of the quilt is a popular light strategy. Accomplish this in a general way by sprinkling light values in the center of the quilt. For a more specific approach, place the lightest values in the center and gradually move toward darker values in successive rows from the center toward the outer edges. The traditional quilt pattern "Trip Around the World" is a good example of this light strategy and its variations.

Kerry Hoffman used this strategy in her quilt "Venetian Ribbons" on page 61 which features strip-pieced triangles and subtle folded ribbons. She achieved the movement of light to dark primarily in the black-and-white prints that are used as a background for the colored ribbons. She used prints that contain more white and very little black for the lighter areas, and print fabrics that have less and less white in them for the darker areas. Since the colored ribbons also darken from the center to the edges of the quilt, they almost seem to disappear as the eye travels around the perimeter of this piece.

Venetian Ribbons (detail) by Kerry Hoffman, 1994, Mercer Island, Washington, 57" x 57". The full quilt is shown opposite.

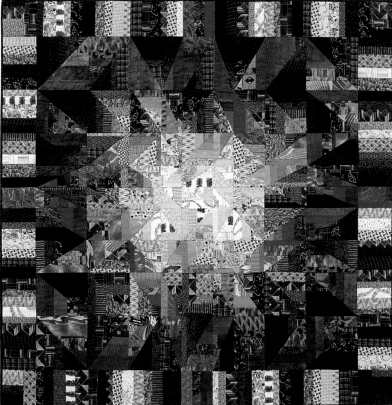

Lent by Marty Kutz, 1994, Sedro Wooley, Washington, 52" x 55". Owned by Mount Vernon Presbyterian Church, Mount Vernon, Washington. This quilt was a challenge for Marty because she doesn't care for purple as a color to work with, but she needed a wall hanging for her church for the Lenten season. Her quilting friends subtitled this quilt "She's Giving Up Purple for Lent . . ."

Venetian Ribbons by Kerry Hoffman, 1994, Mercer Island, Washington, 57" x 57". This quilt is a good example of the "spotlight in the center" color strategy, which is used in both the figure and the ground. Kerry worked with bands of color so they appear to weave over and under each other in the center of the quilt and fold back on themselves at the edges.

Variations on the Basic Light Strategies

To make quilts that "reach for the un-expected," to make the viewer take a second look, you may want to explore variations of the basic light strategies. Take a predictable strategy and make it unpredictable—make standard color and light strategies "sing new songs."

Following are some of the ways to accomplish this. Remember that these strategies are more successful with some Blockbender grids than with others. Sometimes, the light strategies discussed earlier are more effective with the range of fabrics you have chosen and the particular grid with which you are working. Before you commit yourself to any one strategy, consider the variations first.

Rotating the Grid

Take the color strategies you have illustrated with your own fabric squares and rotate them. Sometimes a quilt you have finished looks good "right side up" (or the way you designed it on your design wall), but when you turn it upside down or sideways, it is *stupendous*! This is especially true with Blockbender quilts.

Three-dimensional shapes may emerge from the flat quilt surface when it is turned sideways.

1	1	1	1	1
2	2	2	2	2
3	3	3	3	3
4	4	4	4	4
5	5	5	5	5

1	2	3	4	5
1	2	3	4	5
1	2	3	4	5
1	2	3	4	5
1	2	3	4	5

5	5	5	5	5
4	4	4	4	4
3	3	3	3	3
2	2	2	2	2
1	1	1	1	1

5	4	3	2	1
5	4	3	2	1
5	4	3	2	1
5	4	3	2	1
5	4	3	2	1

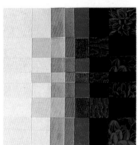

Placing the Focus Off-Center

Think how a quilt may change when the "horizontal band of light" moves down about one-third or one-fourth of the way from the top edge. What happens if you move the vertical shaft of light a little to the left or right of the center? Would the quilt be more interesting if the spotlight were off-center rather than dead-center in the quilt?

6	6	6	6	6	6	6
7	7	7	7	7	7	7
1	1	1	1	1	1	1
2	2	2	2	2	2	2
3	3	3	3	3	3	3
4	4	4	4	4	4	4
5	5	5	5	5	5	5

3	2	1	2	3	4	5
3	2	1	2	3	4	5
3	2	1	2	3	4	5
3	2	1	2	3	4	5
3	2	1	2	3	4	5
3	2	1	2	3	4	5
3	2	1	2	3	4	5

4	3	2	3	4	5	6
3	2	1	2	3	4	5
2	1	1	1	2	3	4
3	2	1	2	3	4	5
4	3	2	3	4	5	6
5	4	3	4	5	6	7
6	5	4	5	6	7	7

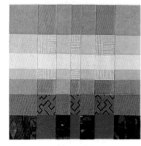
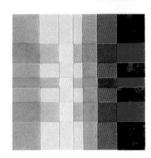

How would it look if the diagonal shaft of light did not extend exactly from corner to corner on a square quilt? On a rectangular quilt, of course, a diagonal shaft of light does not extend from corner to corner exactly.

It looks as though Maggie Worline sprinkled light diagonally across her quilt "Pinwheel Version Two." Though there is a diagonal shaft of light from one corner to the other, the lightest triangles spread like confetti to other "generally central"

areas of the quilt as well. Note how the design shifts from pinwheels to diamonds as the eye travels across the quilt.

Pinwheel Version Two (detail)
by Maggie Worline, 1994, Camano Island, Washington, 30" x 40". The full quilt is shown on page 77.
▼

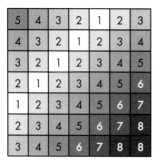

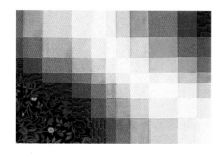

Repeating a Strategy More Than Once

Instead of making the horizontal band of light range from the lightest values at one edge to the darkest values at the opposite edge, place the light values on one edge and move toward the dark values, this time placing them in the middle of the quilt. Then, go abruptly back to light in the middle and move toward the dark in the same sequence again.

Apply this variation to other strategies—the diagonal shaft of light, the light from the corner, and the spotlight in the center. Contrast, which creates visual interest, occurs in the areas where the darkest values meet the lightest ones.

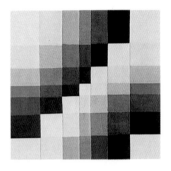

A good example of multiple repeats of lights and darks is in Marguerite McCallion's quilt "Mother Nature." Starting with the center of either sphere, note the rhythm of the dark-light-dark-light repetition of values. The contrast of the dark greens next to the pale blues makes the spheres look like parts of planets floating in space.

Another good example of this repeating light strategy is Flo Peel's quilt "Riley's Star." This quilt is a variation of Grid C; though the light strategy appears to be "spotlight in the center," note how Flo moved from light to dark, then abruptly to light again to form the background of her star motif.

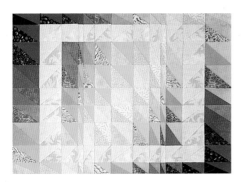

Inner border is much lighter than quilt.

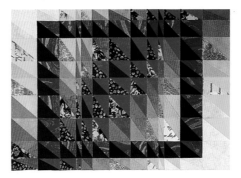

Inner border is much darker than quilt.

Inner border moves from dark to light as quilt moves from light to dark in value.

Inner border forms entirely different motif than in quilt.

An abrupt change in value can also be used to create a border within a border. For instance, in the second to last row on all the quilt's edges, use values that are very pale compared with the rest of the quilt. One way to achieve paleness is to choose very light values in the predominant colors in your quilt, or use the wrong side of the fabrics you have used in the rest of the quilt.

This border-within-a-border visual technique creates an illusion that the outermost units are the border of the quilt. The outside rows also become a "quiet space" to bring the quilt to a gradual visual end.

Try creating a border within a border by using values that are darker than the units in the adjacent rows; or choose colors for the inner border that are complementary to the surrounding colors.

You could also reverse the pattern of light. In a quilt that is generally light at the top and becomes darker toward the bottom, make the border within a border so that it is dark at the top and lighter toward the bottom.

The border within a border need not have straight edges; in my quilt "Trail of Diamonds" on page 49, the spiraling ribbon actually forms a border within a border.

Reversing the Values

Look at any of the light strategies—the basics and the variations, beginning on pages 56 and 64 respectively—and consider reversing the position of the darks and lights.

For example, using the "spotlight in the center" strategy, consider putting your darkest values in the center and gradually move toward lighter values as you approach the borders of the quilt.

1	2	3	4	3	2	1
2	3	4	5	4	3	2
3	4	5	6	5	4	3
4	5	6	6	6	5	4
3	4	5	6	5	4	3
2	3	4	5	4	3	2
1	2	3	4	3	2	1

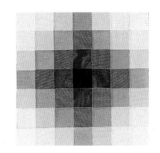

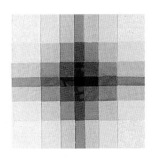

With the "vertical shaft of light strategy," place the lightest values at the edges and move toward darker values in the center.

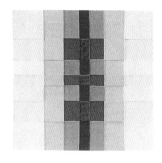

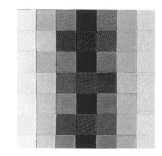

The reversal strategy takes on new meaning when you use Blockbender units instead of squares, as you have practiced up to this point. When you consider the simplest of the line designs presented—that of all diagonal lines going the same direction—you can apply more than one light strategy to the pieced surface. Try using one light strategy in the lower triangles, and another strategy in the upper triangles.

To indicate light strategies on the Blockbender grids, use a different-colored pencil for the numbers in the lower triangles than for those in the upper triangles. By using two colors, you will save time when searching for the proper template and value for any given shape in your quilt design.

For example, considering only the upper triangles of each unit, you could place light values of one color family at the top edge of the quilt and gradually work down to the darkest values at the bottom of the quilt. In the lower triangle of each unit, you could employ the reverse light strategy,

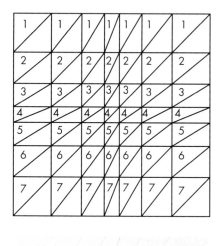

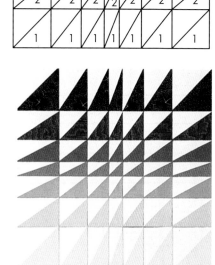

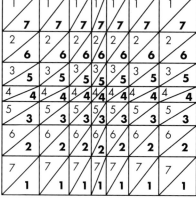

◀ **Beacon Clearing** by Margaret J.
Miller, 1992, Woodinville, Washington, 70½" x 71½". Machine
quilted by Patsi Hanseth, Mount
Vernon, Washington. This quilt
features two "rainbow" colors in
the upper triangles for every
single "gray" fabric in the lower
triangles. In addition, the rainbow goes from light in the center
to dark at the outside edges of
the quilt, while the blacks go
from dark in the center to lighter
grays at the edges.

using another color family. Place your darkest values in the lower triangles of each unit at the top edge of the quilt and gradually place lighter and lighter values in the lower triangles as you approach the bottom edge.

In "Beacon Clearing," I used the "spotlight off-center" light strategy in the upper triangles of each unit. I started with a single triangle of value 1 (the lightest value) slightly off-center. Echo-ing out from the "center" are single rows of each remaining value, with the darkest value located on the outer edges.

In the *lower triangles*, note that the values go from dark in the center to light in the outer ar-eas. Also, there is a double row of each value echoing out from five triangles of the darkest value in the "center."

11/1	10 9 / 2 2	8/3	7/3	6/4	5/4	4/5	5/4	6/4	7/3	8 9 / 3 2	10/2
10/2	9 8 / 2 3	7/3	6/4	5/4	4/5	3/5	4/5	5/4	6/4	7 8 / 3 3	9/2
9/2	8 7 / 3 3	6/4	5/4	4/5	3/5	2/6	3/5	4/5	5/4	6 7 / 4 3	8/3
8/3	7 6 / 3 4	5/4	4/5	3/5	2/6	1/6	2/6	3/5	4/5	5 6 / 5 4	7/3
9/2	8 7 / 3 3	6/4	5/4	4/5	3/5	2/6	3/5	4/5	5/4	6 7 / 4 3	8/3
10/2	9 8 / 2 3	7/3	6/4	5/4	4/5	3/5	4/5	5/4	6/4	7 8 / 3 3	9/2
11/1	10 9 / 2 2	8/3	7/3	6/4	5/4	4/5	5/4	6/4	7/3	8 9 / 3 2	10/2
12/1	11 10 / 1 2	9/2	8/3	7/3	6/4	5/4	6/4	7/3	8/3	9 10 / 2 2	11/1

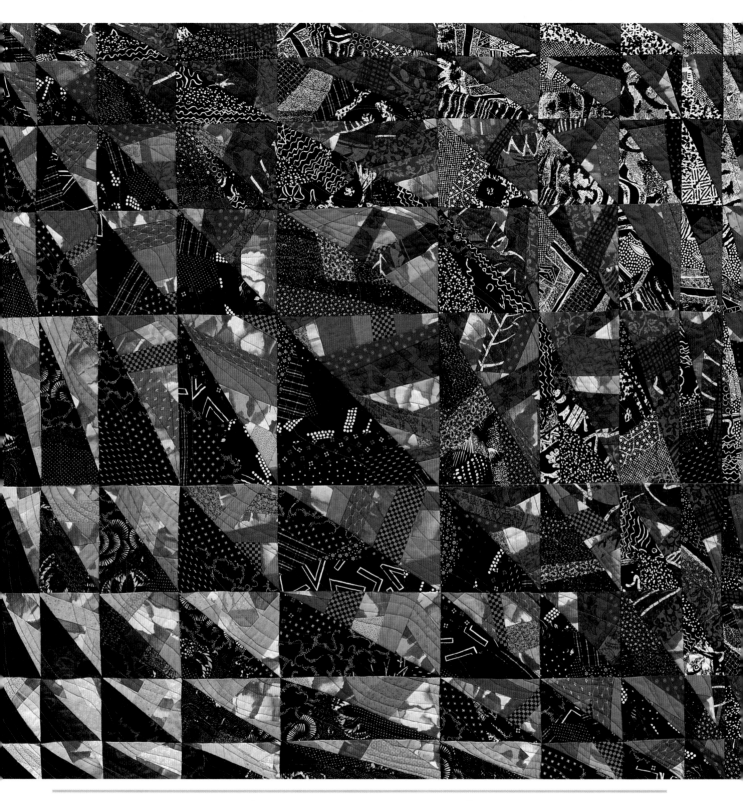

Janet Steadman played with this strategy in her quilt "Crazy Triangles," which she made in 1991, long before I began playing with Blockbender quilts. Note that each of the triangles in this quilt are crazy-patched. The pink triangles transition from light in one corner to dark in the opposite corner. Meanwhile, the black-and-white triangles go from dark to light in the same direction. Note that the two corners that have the highest contrast (upper right and lower left) are what hold the eye in this piece.

Crossing Shafts of Light

This light strategy has multiple possibilities, whether you are working with a pieced surface composed of all squares only or with a more versatile surface of Blockbender triangles.

Crossing shafts of light with single rows of squares or single rows of triangles is relatively simple. But, if you want to have double rows of your values, the crossing in the center presents some challenges, especially with the Blockbender grids. As you can see in the mock-ups below, once you place the crossing shafts of light in the center, you need to fill in the units in all directions—north, south, east, and west. Remember that you need not use the same light strategy "north and south" that you employ "east and west."

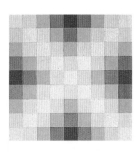 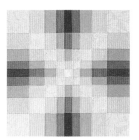

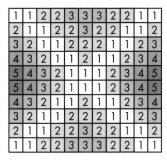 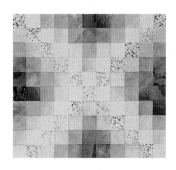 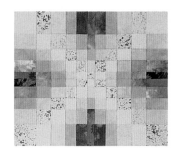

An alternative is to place the "vertical shaft of light" strategy in the lower triangles; in the upper triangles, rotate the vertical shaft of light to make it a horizontal one.

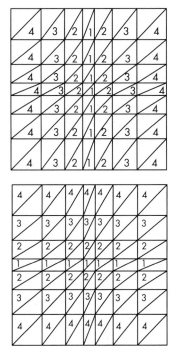 

Remember that the two shafts of light do not have to cross in the center of the pieced surface; try crossing them off-center.

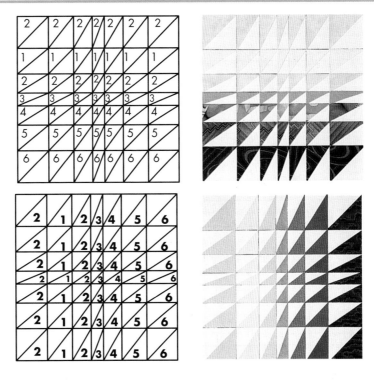

With the "diagonal shaft of light strategy," place the shaft of light corner to corner in the lower triangles. In the upper triangles, place the lightest values in a diagonal line, but somewhere other than corner to corner.

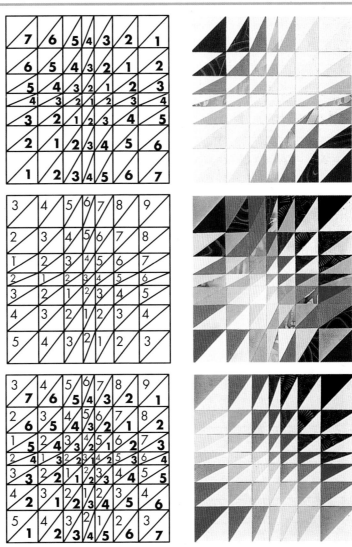

In my quilt "Gaslamp Quarter" below, I used two light strategies. In the lower triangles, a vertical shaft of light is left of center. In the upper triangles, a diagonal shaft of light begins at the fourth triangle from the left on the bottom row and travels up toward the upper right corner of the quilt.

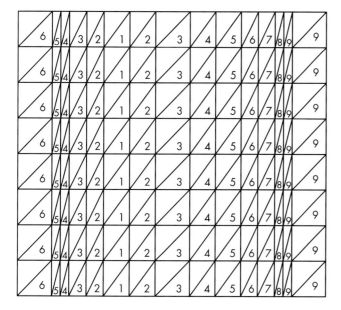

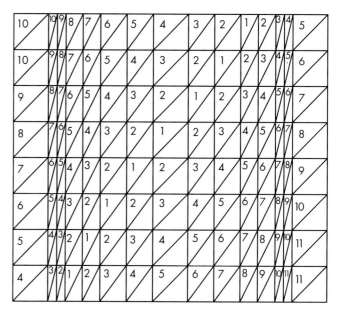

◄ **Gaslamp Quarter** by Margaret J. Miller, 1992, Woodinville, Washington, 70" x 68". Machine quilted by Patsi Hanseth, Mount Vernon, Washington.

Using Partial Strategies

Yet another option is to use a light strategy in either all of the upper *or* lower triangles, then use only one fabric for all of the remaining triangles. This is the strategy employed by Marty Kutz in her quilt "The Colors of Our Skin Are God's Design."

Using Blockbender Grid B, Marty placed a diagonal shaft of light in the lower triangles, extending it from corner to corner and transitioning to dark values at the opposite corners. All of the upper triangles were cut from the same hand-dyed fabric.

The Colors of Our Skin Are God's Design by Marty Kutz, 1994, Sedro Wooley, Washington, 45" x 46½". The center portion of this quilt was complete and hanging on Marty's design wall until she connected its colors with a song written in 1987 by Shirley Erena Murry, "O God, We Bear the Imprint of Your Face." The colors in the quilt then began to represent the skin colors of the peoples of the world. The quilting designs are line drawings of people from the American Bible Society edition of **The Good News Bible.**

▼

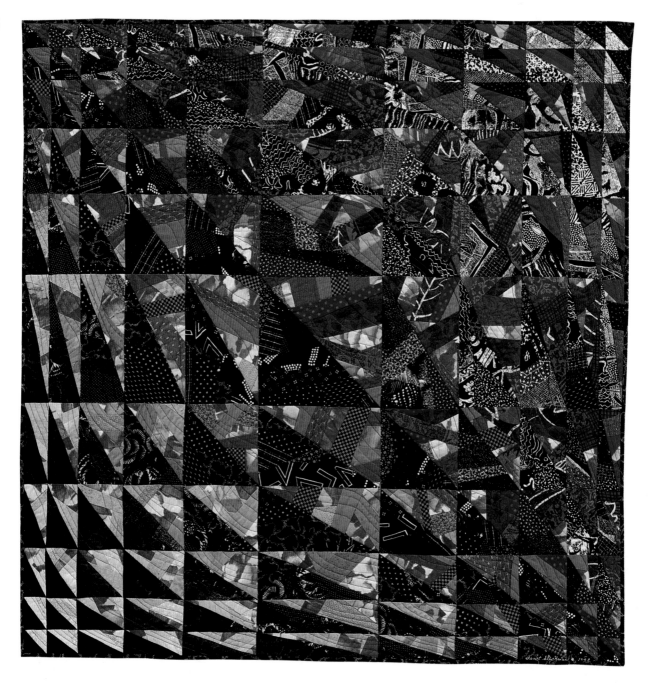

Crazy Triangles by Janet W. Steadman, 1991, Clinton, Washington, 39" x 39". All the triangles in this quilt are crazy-pieced from scrap fabrics. The design was inspired by a picture Janet saw in a Japanese book a few years ago. Though Janet derived many quilt designs from the picture, this is the only quilt that has resulted . . . so far.

Pinwheel Version Two by
Maggie Worline, 1994, Camano
Island, Washington, 30" x 40".
Using the opposing zigzag line
design, Maggie sprinkled her values in such a way that the viewer
sees pinwheels in some parts of
this quilt and quartered diamonds in others.

Playing with Mock-ups

If you have a limited supply of fabric, or if you would like to practice this "light strategy" approach more extensively before cutting your fabrics, play with mock-ups rather than full-size quilts.

You gain a lot of experience with color and value while using real fabric (not colored pencil shadings), and you have framable pieces when you are done. Draw the grid of your choice (any of the grids in Appendix A, beginning on page 131, or one of your own designs) onto graph paper. Remember that the numbers along the edge of the grids refer to the number of squares on 8-squares-per-inch graph paper. Using Grid C as an example, note that the narrowest strip is 4 squares or ½" wide. For your first several mock-ups, do not work with anything smaller than ½".

Make several photocopies of your drawing. In addition, make a photocopy at a reduced scale to use as a template reference. You may want to make a few copies of the reduced drawing so you can make several different-colored patterns using colored pencils.

Once you have settled on a color and light strategy, gather the appropriate fabrics and assign value numbers to them. (1 is the lightest value; the higher the number, the darker the value.) Adhere swatches (about 9" x 9") of each fabric to paper-backed fusible web (I prefer Wonder-Under®), following the manufacturer's directions exactly. Do not remove the paper backing yet.

You will use rotary-cutting techniques to cut rectangles and squares, then crosscut them to fill in your photocopied grid with triangles. To determine the strip widths to cut from the prepared fabric, measure the widths on your photocopied grid. Be sure to measure from your photocopied grid (not your original graph-paper grid), since photocopying distorts original drawings somewhat. Note the measurements in the margins of the photocopy.

Referring to the noted measurements, cut one strip from each fabric. For example, with Grid C, cut one strip in each of the following widths from each fabric: 1¼", 1", ¾", ½". Write the value number at the end of each fabric strip for easy reference.

Arrange the strips in order on your table by value number. It is helpful to paper clip each fabric grouping together, so when you are ready to cut a square or rectangle from the strip, you can fan out the strips and cut what you need from the end of a single strip width.

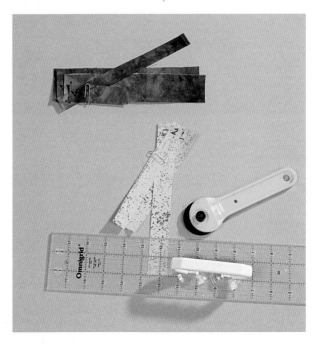

To save time and for greater accuracy, cut a square or rectangle of the appropriate size from the strip, then cut the square or rectangle once diagonally to yield triangles. An alternative method is to make templates for each of the triangles needed, but this method is less accurate and more difficult. Cut triangles from the appropriate numbered values and adhere them to your photocopied grid according to the light strategy you have chosen.

As you cut triangles for your photocopied grid, set aside the extra triangle on a piece of paper (your "tray"), which you have numbered to match the size of your Blockbender grid units. If the fabrics you are using are close in value, write the value number on the back of the loose triangle for future reference. Some of the "spare" triangles will be used elsewhere in the same mock-up or, perhaps, in another mock-up in the same series.

To adhere triangles, peel the paper backing from the back of the fabric and gently tack in place on the photocopied drawing with your iron. I find that I maintain greater accuracy (and burn my fingers less often) by using a travel iron on a firm ironing surface—I use a travel ironing board. Be sure to cover the background paper completely; no white paper should show between fabric pieces.

Once all the triangles have been tacked in place, take the mock-up to your regular ironing board. (Be sure it has a *firm* surface.) Place mock-up right side down and complete the adhesion process, using a very hot, dry, full-size iron. Keep the iron moving over the paper so you don't make any "iron track" marks on the mock-up.

Some people like to adhere all of the lower triangles in place first, then choose the upper triangles. Others like to place all the triangles on the drawing before adhering any of them. Whichever approach you use, remember: don't agonize; jump in and cut all the triangles quickly, then fine-tune your value choices later!

More Uses for the Number System

Assigning a set of numbers to a given selection of fabrics is useful in a variety of ways. To grade values from light to dark evenly over a quilt surface, simply write numbers sequentially on shapes that occur in a pattern across the paper design. The agony of choosing fabrics for your quilt is eliminated, since you are merely substituting fabrics with their assigned numbers.

I have found four other ways to use the numbering system. You will undoubtedly find more.

Using More than Two Color Families

You may wish to use the number system to add additional color families to your quilt. Refer to the color wheel and the system developed by Johannes Itten and presented in Appendix B on page 141.

Choose the color families, then pull all the fabrics you have in those color families from your collection. Be sure you have a complete range of value (from very light to very dark) in each of the color families. Cut a

swatch of each fabric and glue it to a swatch sheet, assigning a number to each fabric. Remember to use a different-colored pencil to write the numbers for each color family and use the assigned colors on your drawings.

Separating the Figure from the Background

You may wish to use more than one light strategy in a quilt design that has figures (such as interlocking open rectangles) against a background. In the figures, you may move from dark values in the center to light values at the edges of the quilt. In the background behind the figures, use the opposite strategy—go from light in the center to dark at the outside edges. This approach separates the figure from the background dramatically.

A variation of this strategy is to keep the values of the figure constant and change the light strategy of the background as shown at right.

See Bonnie Mitchell's quilt "Diamonds" on page 45 for an example of this light strategy using strip-pieced triangles. First, study the diamond network. Notice that the diamond in the center is dark and that the diamonds get lighter as the eye moves toward the outer edges of the quilt. The background be-

hind the diamonds is very light in the center and gets darker toward the edges.

Donna Holthusen used the same light strategy in her quilt "Nova," on page 82, which is made of strip-pieced triangles.

The separation of figure from background is very different from Bonnie's "Diamonds" quilt because many values are included in each triangle. The result is a much more subtle movement of dark toward light.

Nova by Donna Holthusen, 1994, Everett, Washington, 56" x 63". Using an extended version of Grid C and a radiating line design, Donna used oranges to browns opposite blues in the triangles of this quilt. Ribbons of color in broken and unbroken bands radiate out from the central star.

Rainbow Flow by Vivian Heiner, 1994, Seattle, Washington, 26" x 21". Using a color strategy in which the upper triangles go around the color wheel, and the lower triangles remain in shades of gray, Vivian maximized the feeling of triangles flowing over an undulating surface.

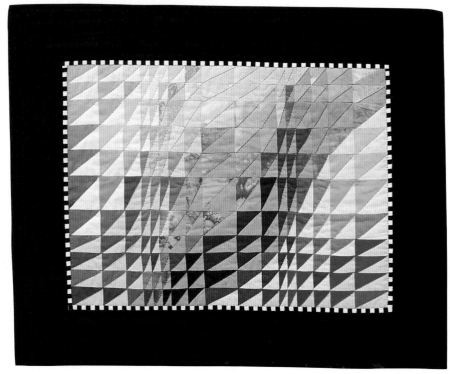

Creating Bands of Color

Another option is to choose a single value (mediums or lights, for example) and go around the color wheel to achieve your fabric palette.

Assign numbers as before, but instead of assigning numbers to values, assign them to each color. Then, if your design is diagonal bands across the quilt, each diagonal band could begin with a different-colored number, thus producing a rainbow of color across the quilt surface.

Vivian Heiner used this approach in her quilt "Rainbow Flow." In the lower triangles, diagonal streams of four different gray fabrics flow from corner to corner across the surface. In the upper triangles, the color moves around the color wheel, from red to yellow, to green, to blue, to purple, and back to red again, as the eye travels from the upper left corner of the quilt to the lower right one.

A variation on this theme would be to use a range of colors (for example, yellow-orange through red to purple) and, in addition, vary the values of those fabrics from very light to very dark. By assigning a single number to each fabric, you can easily sprinkle light and multiple fabrics across the quilt surface.

Mockup based on swatch sheet above.

Using Sequential Motifs

If you develop a quilt design that features sequential motifs (for example, the braided pattern shown here), you could assign sets of numbers to *like units,* which would make the shapes either darken gradually or transform color as the eye moves across the surface of the quilt. In the example below, three colors next to each other on the color wheel (analogous colors) were selected—yellows through greens to blues. The number "1" was assigned to the first yellow, and the number "12" represents the last blue in the series.

Like units

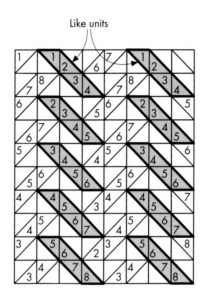

Like units

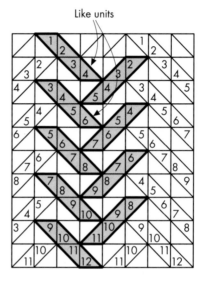

Making a Blockbender Quilt

The process of making a Blockbender quilt is a relatively straightforward one, since only one shape, a right triangle, is involved. The first step is to develop a line design.

To demonstrate the process, I selected Grid C with the following line design. The quilt in this chapter is made using single-fabric triangles. A quilt with strip-pieced triangles appears in the next chapter.

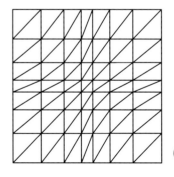

C

Choosing a Size

The chart below shows the finished sizes of quilts made using Grids A through I. The numbers indicated on the edges of the grids represent the unit's measurements in inches. Based on Grid C, a finished quilt (excluding borders) using "full-size" templates measures 52" x 52". This appears in the "Full Size" column in the chart below. Referring to Grid C in Appendix A on page 133, note that the unit sizes are 10", 8", 6", and 4"—the sizes that appear along the edges of the grid.

Quilt Sizes (Width x Length in inches)

Grid	Full Size	Three-Quarter Size	Half Size	Quarter Size
A	52 x 52	39 x 39	26 x 26	13 x 13
B	46 x 68	34.5 x 51.0	23 x 34	11.5 x 17.0
C	52 x 52	39 x 39	26 x 26	13 x 13
D	72 x 60	54 x 45	36 x 30	18 x 15
E	72 x 64	54 x 48	36 x 32	18 x 16
F	60 x 56	45 x 42	30 x 28	15 x 14
G	80 x 56	60 x 42	40 x 28	20 x 14
H	54 x 64	40.5 x 48.0	27 x 32	13.5 x 16.0
I	58 x 58	43.5 x 43.5	29 x 29	14.5 x 14.5

Note that some of the "full-size" grids will make some very large quilts. Grid D, for instance, makes a quilt that is 72" x 60". Suppose you want to use Grid D, but you don't want such a large quilt. Look at the figures for Grid D in the "Three-Quarter Size" column (54" x 45"), then in the "Half Size" column (36" x 30"). Perhaps a quilt made in these smaller sizes would be more realistic.

Note that the measurements in the "Quarter Size" column are extremely small to make in fabric, unless you are a miniature enthusiast and highly skilled at accurately sewing tiny units with multiple angles. This size is ideal for making Blockbender mock-ups, however.

Making Blockbender Quilt Templates

Once you have selected a finished size for your grid design, make a list of the templates you will need. Since each square or rectangular unit in a Blockbender quilt is divided in half diagonally, the two resulting triangles are identical. Therefore, only one triangular template is needed per unit. Since some of the units are repeated, you may need a relatively small number of templates to make a Blockbender quilt.

The first step is to draft the triangle shapes (finished size, without seam allowances) onto graph paper. The templates will be made from template plastic at a later stage in the process.

Beginning in the upper left

corner of your grid, make a list of the triangle sizes you need row by row. For a full-size quilt, using Grid C as an example, make triangle templates in the following unit sizes: 10" x 10", 10" x 8", 10" x 6", and 10" x 4".

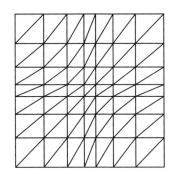
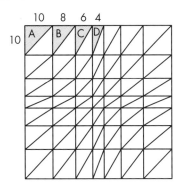

Notice that the three units on the right side of the top row are identical to the first three units in our template list.

Next, go to the second row. The first triangle size is 8" x 10", but since you have already listed that size, you don't need to list it again (a 10" x 8" triangle can be rotated so that it is 8" x 10"). Working across the row, add the following triangles to your list: 8" x 8", 8" x 6", and 8" x 4".

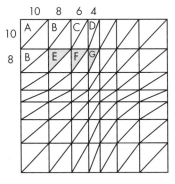

Continue adding to the list, row by row, until you have listed all the triangles needed to make a Blockbender quilt from Grid C. The completed list is:

10" x 10"	8" x 8"	6" x 6"	4" x 4"
10" x 8"	8" x 6"	6" x 4"	
10" x 6"	8" x 4"		
10" x 4"			

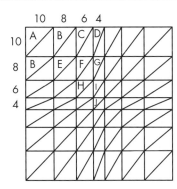

It is sometimes surprising to note how few templates some of the Blockbender grids require. In Grid E, for example, since the horizontal lines are all equidistant from each other, only four templates are required: 8" x 8", 8" x 6", 8" x 4", and 8" x 2".

Drafting and cutting triangle templates must be done carefully to ensure accurate results. It is important to understand that the diagonal seam of each different rectangular unit intersects the outside edge (cut edge) of the template shape at a different distance from the outside corner. The diagonal line intersects the corners of the seam line *and* the corners of the outside edge in square units only.

Therefore, you must use great care in making templates. With properly made templates and careful piecing techniques, your diagonal seams will intersect the corners of the Blockbender units perfectly.

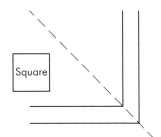
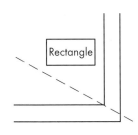

Triangle Templates

The method for making templates described here was developed by Libby Leman of Houston, Texas. Her article on this method was published in *American Quilter* magazine (Summer 1993, Vol. IX, No. 2, page 58) just as I was beginning to make the first Blockbender quilts. The timing of the article was providential, as it is a perfect system for making Blockbender triangles.

Few supplies are needed to make Blockbender templates. I use template plastic, ¼"-wide masking tape, a long plastic gridded ruler, and graph paper (8 squares per inch).

I keep two rotary cutters in the studio. One has a sharp blade for cutting fabric, and the other has a blade that is too dull for that purpose but is useful for cutting template plastic, cardboard, and paper.

Save your templates and use them to make another Blockbender quilt, since many quilts can be designed from the same grid. All full-size grids are based on the same dimensions: 2", 4", 6", 8", and 10".

1. On graph paper, carefully draw each of the triangles you need for your quilt. In the chart that follows, you will find relative sizes of templates for making full-size, three-quarter-size, half-size, or quarter-size quilts.

Unit Size (Squares and Rectangles) on Grids			
Full Size	Three-Quarter Size	Half Size	Quarter Size
12	9	6	3
10	7.5	5	2.5
8	6	4	2
6	4.5	3	1.5
4	3	2	1
2	1.5	1	0.5

Continuing the use of Grid C as an example, to make a quilt based on this grid at three-quarter size, draft the following triangular templates, instead of the full-size ones listed before:

7.5 x 7.5	6 x 6	4.5 x 4.5	3 x 3
7.5 x 6	6 x 4.5	4.5 x 3	
7.5 x 4.5	6 x 3		
7.5 x 3			

When you are drawing these shapes, be sure to allow plenty of space around them, because you will be adding seam allowances and some of the triangles will have very elongated points. You don't want to run off the edge of the paper.

2. It is helpful to draw a "half-diagonal" seam onto each template, using a red pencil. This seam is necessary for folded ribbon designs, for example. On your graph paper, find the "missing corner" of your square or rectangular unit. Place your ruler diagonally across the triangle from this point to the opposite corner. Draw the line within the triangle only.

3. Use a gridded ruler to add a ¼"-wide seam allowance to each side of the drafted triangle.

Check to make sure that the drafted ¼" is the same as the width of your ¼"-wide masking tape. If your masking tape is slightly wider or slightly narrower than the drafted ¼", place your ruler consistently on one edge or the other of your pencil line to compensate for the difference.

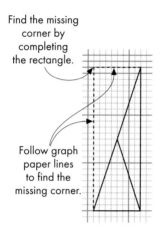

Find the missing corner by completing the rectangle.

Follow graph paper lines to find the missing corner.

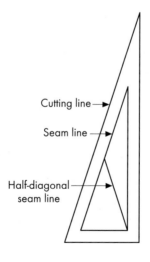

Cutting line

Seam line

Half-diagonal seam line

4. Place template plastic over your graph-paper drawing. Again, allow a healthy margin of plastic around the drafted triangle. Tape the graph paper and template plastic to your cutting table so nothing slips during this process.

5. To establish the seam allowances on the template plastic, anchor one end of the ¼"-wide masking tape first, then carefully align one edge of the masking tape with the sewing line of the drafted triangle underneath. Extend the masking tape well beyond the points of the triangle.

6. Trace the red half-diagonal line (drawn in step 2) from the graph paper onto your template. Separate the template plastic from the graph paper and trim away the plastic that extends beyond the outer edge of the masking tape. The masking tape is now your seam allowance. For best results, always place the triangular template under the Plexiglas straightedge and cut from the elongated point of the triangle toward the base of the triangle.

7. Place the plastic template next to the graph-paper drawing of the triangle so the two shapes form a rectangle. Then, turn the template over on top of the drawn triangle, as though you were sewing two pieces of fabric right sides together to form a rectangle. Align the seam lines to make sure that you placed the tape accurately. The diagonal seam line of the drawn triangle should fit the "window" within the masking tape exactly.

Look at the points at each end of the diagonal line of the triangle—one point is elongated,

Steps 2 and 3

Step 4

Step 5

Step 6

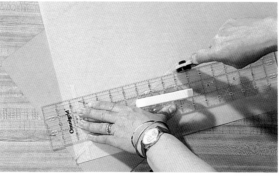

Step 6

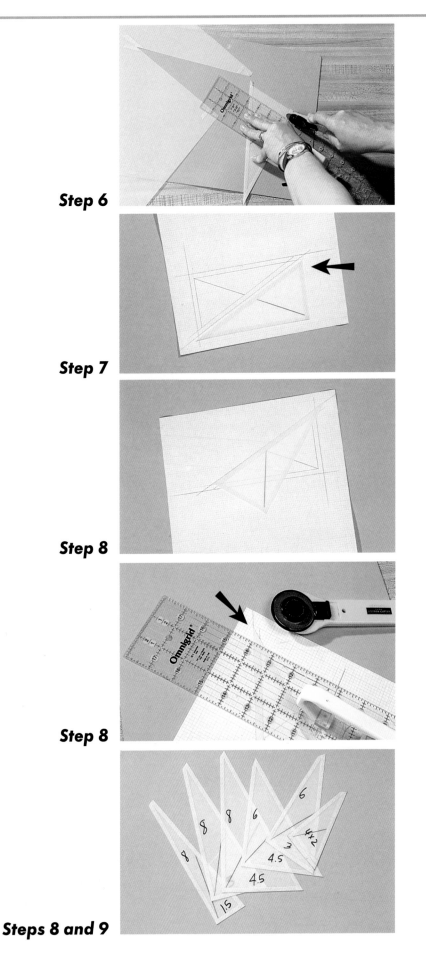

Step 6

Step 7

Step 8

Step 8

Steps 8 and 9

the other is more blunt. On the elongated end, the point extends well beyond the cutting line drawn on the graph paper. At the other end, the plastic does not extend beyond the cutting line.

8. Trace the cutting line that you see through the elongated point onto the plastic template from the graph paper below. Trim away excess plastic beyond this line.

You will trim away more plastic on some triangles, less on others. Also, every different triangle will have its point cut at a different angle. *Trim accurately* to ensure that triangles will fit together precisely. Triangles that are half of a square need no trimming.

9. Clearly label the size of your template.

Square and Rectangle Templates

To ensure that your fabric blocks are cut and sewn accurately, make a set of square and rectangle templates to check the size and shape of your blocks before you sew them together into rows. Follow the same procedure for making templates as described above; however, no final trimming is necessary. Be sure to mark one corner-to-corner diagonal line on each square or rectangle template.

Quarter-Unit Triangle Templates

If your design involves half diagonals (page 38) or crossed diagonals (page 42), it is helpful to make two "quarter-unit" triangle templates (A and B) for the blocks that require them. These are in addition to the half-unit template (C) described on pages 88–90.

Follow the same procedure for making templates A and B as you did for template C. Draw a grain line on templates A and B to indicate which edge you want to place on the fabric's straight of grain. Label each triangle with the dimensions of the square or rectangle of which it is a part.

I use these templates for "rough cutting" fabrics only. After deciding on the appropriate fabrics, cut out and sew the two "rough cut" triangles together. Then place the triangle template over the two-fabric unit, align-

ing the seam with the red half-diagonal line marked on the template. Finally, trace around the template and cut out the triangle.

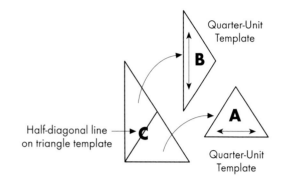

Half-diagonal line on triangle template — **C**

Quarter-Unit Template — **B**

A — Quarter-Unit Template

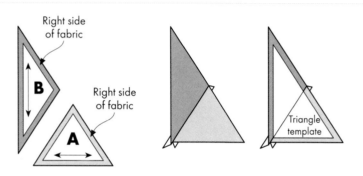

Right side of fabric — **B**

Right side of fabric — **A**

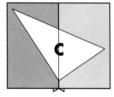

Triangle template

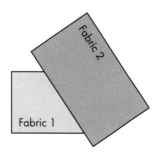

C — Align red half-diagonal line with the seam of two joined fabric strips.

You can also sew two fabric strips, rather than two triangles together, then align the red half-diagonal line with the seam. Trace and cut.

Here is another method for joining quarter-unit triangles.

1. Place quarter-unit template A on fabric 1 so the edge that represents the bottom of the rectangle is on the straight of grain. Align your cutting ruler with the side of the triangle to

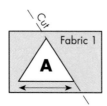

Cut

Fabric 1 — **A**

which you will be sewing fabric 2; cut.

2. With right sides together, sew a piece of fabric 2 to fabric 1, aligning it with the just-cut edge of fabric 1. Press.

Fabric 2

Fabric 1

Fabric 1

3. Place triangle template C on the just-sewn two-fabric unit, aligning the seam with the red diagonal line marked on the template. Trace and cut.

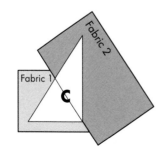

Fabric 2

Fabric 1

C

Marking Fabrics and Cutting Triangles

Now you are ready to begin cutting triangles from your fabrics and placing them on your design wall. Keep your numbered fabric swatch sheet and your numbered line drawing close at hand for easy reference.

Using your line drawing as a guide, choose the appropriate template and trace around it onto the right side of the fabric. If you are using single-fabric triangles, cut several like triangles at once. Stack all fabrics *right side up*. Be sure to accurately trim the tips of the triangles so that they will line up perfectly when you sew them together.

Once all the triangles have been cut and placed on the design wall, it is time to fine-tune your fabric choices. For example, when I cut out the triangles for "Carousel," below, I discovered that using only one fabric for value 1 (the lightest fabric) was too harsh. So I chose another fabric of the same value and alternated the two fabrics in the triangles labeled "1."

It is important to cut *all* the triangles and place them on the design wall *before* you decide on your design. Do not agonize about fabric decisions while you are in the process of cutting the first set of triangles. After all, a triangle that seems to be "wrong" for a given space may turn out to be a good fabric choice, once all the neighboring triangles are put in place. Use your reducing glass to fine-tune your design.

Sewing Triangles Together

Consistent ¼"-wide seams are essential to accurately piece triangles. Use a ¼" quiltmaking presser foot on your machine, or mark on the throat plate a ¼"-wide sewing guide that matches the ¼"-wide seam allowance on your templates.

To save time, chain-piece the triangles together, assembly-line fashion. Start with the left-hand row of triangles.

1. Place a straight pin in the uppermost triangle, parallel to the top edge. This pin will remind you "which end is up" once the row of triangles is sewn and pressed.

2. Place the top two triangles (A and B) right sides together, aligning the long (bias) edges; pin as necessary to control the bias. Sew the pieces together. Do *not* clip the threads until later. Pin and sew the next pair of triangles (C and D) together in the same manner.

3. Continue sewing pairs of triangles together until you've sewn all the units in a vertical row. Press seams open. Clip the "chain" of stitches between the pairs of triangles. Place the completed units on your design wall in the proper order and orientation.

Before sewing the squares and rectangles into rows, be sure to check the accuracy of your sewing and cutting—especially on your first Blockbender quilt. Place the appropriate square or rectangle template on your assembled square or rectangle unit. Align the diagonal line marked on the square/rectangle template with the diagonal seam line. Trim the block as necessary. This step is especially important if your quilt includes very narrow rectangles (1" or 2" wide in one direction) or many units with crossed diagonals.

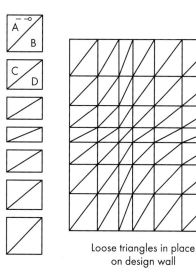

Loose triangles in place
on design wall

Sewing Units to Rows and Rows to Rows

Sew the rows of square and rectangle units together in assembly-line fashion as well.

1. Place a straight pin in the upper left-hand unit, parallel to the left edge, to mark the "top left side" corner of the quilt.

2. With right sides facing, sew units A and B together from top to bottom. Do not clip threads. Sew units C and D together in the same manner from top to bottom. Do not clip threads. Continue until the entire first two vertical rows of blocks are sewn together. *Do not press yet.*

3. Sew unit O to the right-hand side of unit AB, top to bottom. Without cutting threads, sew unit P to unit CD, and so on, until the third vertical row of units is sewn to the first two rows.

4. Continue sewing vertical rows in this fashion until all units are stitched together. Press seam allowances in one direction in all the even-numbered rows; press all seam allowances in the opposite direction in all odd-numbered rows. With this technique, the seam allowances will be "opposing," which makes it easier to match the seams when you sew the rows together.

An alternative is to press seam allowances open, as you did for the diagonal seams.

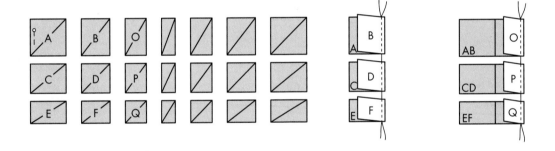

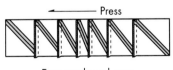

Press ←

Even-numbered rows

Press →

Odd-numbered rows

Strips That Sizzle Meet Blockbender Quilts

Up to this point, we have considered single-fabric triangles in designing Blockbender quilts.

The variables we have manipulated are:

- Various grids based on combinations of square, horizontal, and vertical rectangular units
- The direction of the diagonal within each unit
- The number of color families used
- The number of values used

By replacing single-fabric triangles with strip-pieced triangles, you can add a whole new world of color-blending possibilities to this quilt-design system.

In this chapter, you will substitute strip-pieced triangles for the single-fabric ones discussed earlier. To keep the options to a reasonable number, you will orient the strips so that they are parallel to the outside edges of the block (not to the diagonal)

and perpendicular to each other in each unit.

NOT

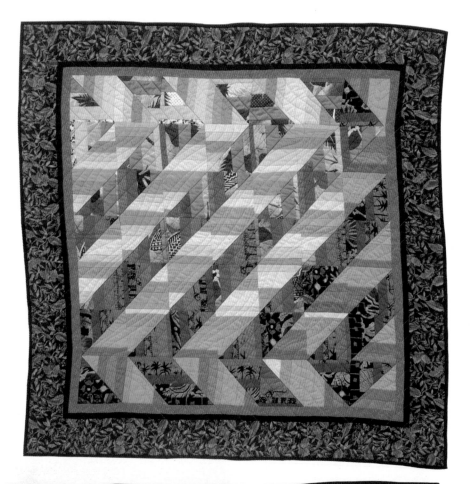

My earlier book, *Strips That Sizzle* (That Patchwork Place), presented many quilts based on square grids. The quilts that are based on squares (not the ones based on on-point blocks) in that book can be "reinterpreted" as Blockbender quilts!

Reynola Pakusich did precisely that with her quilts "Strips That Sizzle" and "Blockbender Interpretation." Note that an ordinary zigzag line in a Strips That Sizzle pattern becomes a billowing line in its Blockbender version.

Any "all-squares" quilt design in the *Strips That Sizzle* book can be made nine different ways, using the nine Blockbender grids in Appendix A, beginning on page 131. Just imagine the surprising new turns Strips That Sizzle quilts will take when applied to the Blockbender quilt grids!

When you look at the Strips That Sizzle quilts, not for their color but for their line design, you will recognize all the line designs we worked with in "Basic Line Designs," beginning on page 12—one-way diagonals, two-way diagonals, parallel zig-

◀ **Strips That Sizzle,** above left (48" x 48"), and **Blockbender Interpretation,** left (51" x 51"), by Reynola Pakusich, 1994, Bellingham, Washington. These quilts are outstanding examples of the way straight paths of color in Strips That Sizzle quilts can become billowing, blowing ribbons in their Blockbender counterparts.

zags, opposing zigzags, and so on. When you combine the strip-pieced approach of Strips That Sizzle with the Blockbender quilt grids, you add other design variables: the shading of light to dark within each triangle and the direction of the strips within the triangles. For example, using the line design in which all diagonals are going the same direction within the grid, you have the following block-orientation possibilities for any given unit.

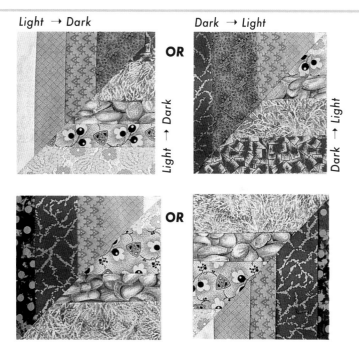

In a color experiment shown here, a set of Strips That Sizzle blocks were placed on the design wall so that a diagonal shaft of light falls across the quilt. Notice that this was done first with all the diagonal seams going in the same direction. (The example below is a fabric mockup using pairs of single-fabric triangles to represent Strips That Sizzle blocks.)

In all the other variations shown, the blocks remain in the same relative position, but by rotating the blocks in place, you create different line designs. Very different color patterns result from one arrangement to the next. Imagine the multitudes of quilt designs that are possible when you consider using the nine Blockbender grids!

Getting Started

Adding strip-pieced triangles makes visualizing a Blockbender quilt quite a bit more complex. There are many more visual options and, thus, more decisions to make. Don't overwhelm yourself by trying to make all decisions at once and remain flexible with the decisions you do make. For example, you may start out with a strong idea about a design or light strategy, but the resulting quilt may not execute this idea at all.

Follow the step-by-step procedure below and try a simpler rather than a more complex design for your first strip-pieced Blockbender quilt. Once you've been through the process, it won't seem so daunting when you make your next quilt! It is very helpful, however, if you spend some time playing with a set of Strips That Sizzle blocks before you begin.

Making a Set of Strips That Sizzle Blocks

Once you have a motif and light pattern established on paper, a set of Strips That Sizzle blocks can be a handy aid in cutting your Blockbender triangles. It is not necessary to make the same number of Strips That Sizzle blocks as you plan to have in your Blockbender quilt; make only 24 or 30 blocks, using six to eight values in each of two color families. Follow the guidelines in *Strips That Sizzle*. These blocks can be rearranged to portray various areas of your Blockbender quilt design. After your Blockbender quilt top is completed, incorporate your Strips That Sizzle blocks into the border or backing. Or, make another quilt top!

Play with your Strips That Sizzle blocks to develop design ideas for the grid you have chosen. Take photographs of each of your arrangements. These snapshots will serve as inspiration for future quilts. As you review your snapshots, rotate them so you are looking at the quilt sideways and upside down; the pattern may be more striking when oriented differently.

Drawing the Line Design

Draw the Strips That Sizzle pattern you like onto a traditional grid (use one of your photocopies of pages 131–39). Then draw this pattern onto one (or several) of the Blockbender grids. Remember that you can continue the same pattern across the entire Blockbender grid or change it from one area of the quilt to another.

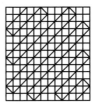

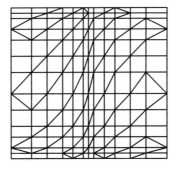

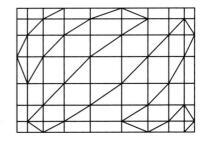

Label each square in your line design with an "L" or a "D," depending on whether it represents a "light" Strips That Sizzle block or a "dark" one. To determine the value, look at the longest strips in the blocks. If the longest strips are light values, they are in a light (L) block; if the longest strips are dark values, they are in a dark (D) block. Note that the letter should be placed in the corner of the square where the long strips come together (at the bend in the L). Some people find it helpful to lightly shade in the dark blocks; I prefer to use letters only, with a line at the edge of the triangle where the long strips should be. I use different-colored pencils to indicate the light and dark blocks. Both approaches are illustrated below.

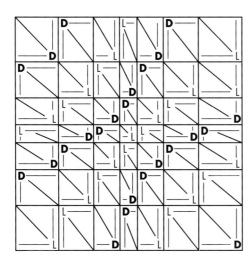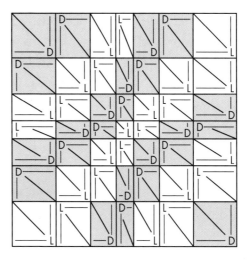

Cutting the Fabrics

For strip-pieced triangles, you will be working with more than six or eight values. Choose at least twelve to fifteen values from very light to very dark in two color families. Make a swatch sheet as described on page 100.

Working with one color family at a time, arrange fabrics from light to dark. Fold fabrics selvage to selvage, stacking two or three folded fabrics on top of each other with the folds offset by about ¼". This makes it easier to separate your strips by fabric later.

Cut along the folds to about 12" from the raw edge. Make two crosscuts of each of the following widths: 2½", 2¼", 2", 1¾", 1½". Lay your cut strips, arranged light to dark, on a surface within easy reach of your sewing machine.

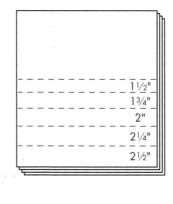

Sewing Strips Together and Making a Swatch Sheet

You will find that doing all of your strip piecing before you cut any triangles saves time. It is frustrating when you discover that you haven't made a particular strip grouping that you want to use in a given triangle. You have to interrupt your work at the design wall to sew that grouping of strips.

Choosing strip widths at random, be sure to include a variety of wide and narrow strips in each grouping of strips; sew four groupings of five strips together in numerical (value) order, starting with value 1. This strip grouping is represented by number 1 on your line design.

Next, beginning with value 2, sew four groupings of values 2 through 6 together. Then, sew values 3 through 7 together. Continue in this manner until you have sewn four of each strip grouping.

```
1 2 3 4 5
 2 3 4 5 6
  3 4 5 6 7
   4 5 6 7 8
    5 6 7 8 9
     6 7 8 9 10
      7 8 9 10 11
       8 9 10 11 12
```

Press all seams in one direction, toward the darker values. Press from the wrong side first, then from the right side, to make sure there are no "bubbles" between the strips or puckers around the seams.

As you sew the groupings together, make a numbered swatch sheet of your strip groupings on a piece of poster board. Your swatch sheet will be an invaluable reference as you begin to translate your numbered drawing into fabric on the design wall.

The number of the lightest value in the group is the number that appears in the light blocks on your line drawing. To represent the dark blocks, use either the number of the darkest value in the group (and shade the block), or the number of the lightest value in the group with a circle around it.

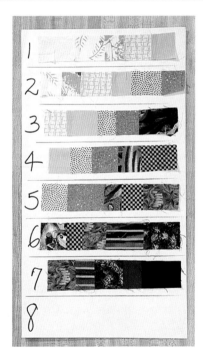

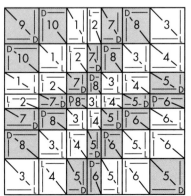

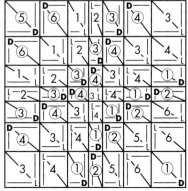

I used the latter system to number the background blocks in my quilt "Trail of Diamonds" on page 49. The shading in the line drawing below highlights the folded ribbon in the inner border.

Note that some triangles are duplicates. For example, if you have twelve values in all and five strips sewn into each grouping, the light block that starts with value 4 is actually the same strip grouping as the one needed for the dark block that starts with value 8.

1 2 3 4 5

　2 3 4 5 6

　　3 4 5 6 7

　　　4 5 6 7 8

　　　　5 6 7 8 9

　　　　　6 7 8 9 10

　　　　　　7 8 9 10 11

　　　　　　　8 9 10 11 12

This will not pose a problem in the design of the quilt because, in a Blockbender quilt, not all the triangles are the same dimension; that is, the light block might measure 6" on a side and the dark block next to it only 2", so you won't be seeing the same number of strips from each of these groupings anyway.

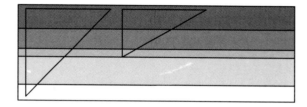

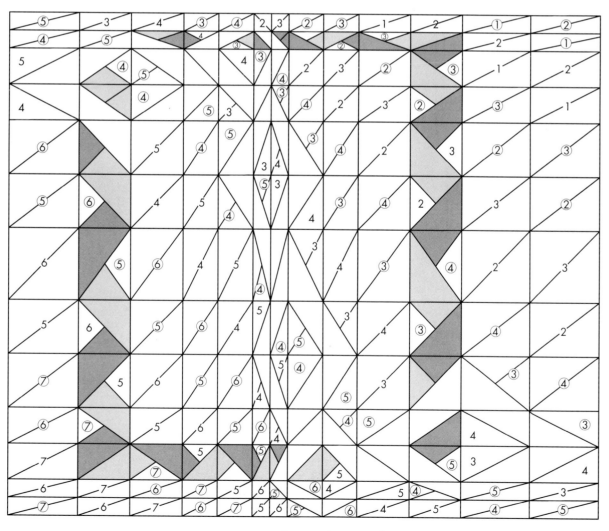

Cutting the Triangles

Strip-pieced triangles must be cut one at a time, because the location of the long strip is important. In addition, the strip-pieced seams must be parallel to the edge of the unit. Make templates as described on pages 88–90.

1. Using your Strips That Sizzle blocks and your line drawing as a guide, note which side of the triangle is lined up with the longest strip and cut your triangle accordingly.

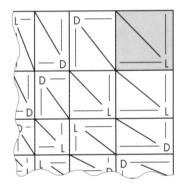

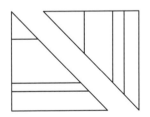

I usually hold the appropriate template up to the design wall, placing my thumb and index finger on the edge of the template where I want the long strip to be. Then I place the template on the strip grouping, with the "thumb edge" of the template oriented along a long strip. Trace the template and use a rotary cutter to cut out on the traced line.

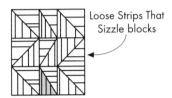

Loose Strips That Sizzle blocks

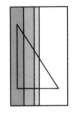

2. Cut a number of triangles and place them on your design wall. Study them, noting how your strip groupings are working in the light strategy you have chosen. This gives you an idea of which strip groupings should be paired together in any given unit (square or rectangle). You will then be able to cut the appropriate diagonal on corresponding pairs of strips, sew them together, and trace and cut out a rectangular shape from the strip groupings already sewn together.

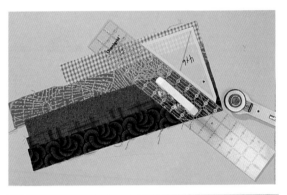

Step 2a: *With strip-pieced grouping right sides up, align side edge of triangular template along desired fabric strip. Place Plexiglas straightedge along diagonal seam edge; cut.*

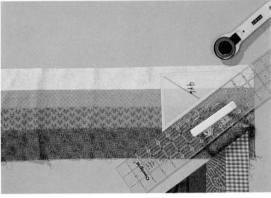

Step 2b: *Place template on corresponding strip grouping, aligning other side edge of template on the value that you want as the longest strip. Cut along diagonal seam edge.*

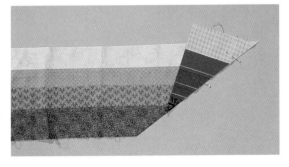

Step 2c: *Sew corresponding triangles together along diagonal seam; press seam open.*

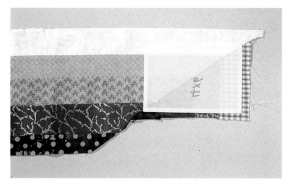

Step 2d: *Place rectangular template on assembled triangles, aligning seam with diagonal on template.*

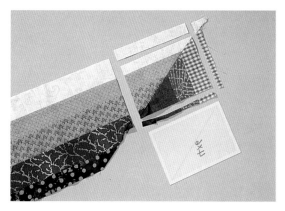

Step 2e: *Trace and cut.*

3. Sew strip-pieced triangles together in the same manner as shown for single-fabric triangles on pages 93–94. Be sure the width of the seam allowance marked (or taped) on your template matches the seam-allowance guide on your sewing machine (or the ¼" quiltmaking foot). Because you are working with bias edges and multiple seams, you may find it helpful to use more pins to hold the triangles together as you sew.

You do not want to stretch the bias edges! You will have better results if you feed the triangle pairs together as shown and sew more carefully than you do when you are doing lots of strip piecing. Press the seams open.

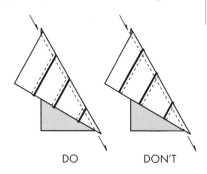

DO   DON'T

Sew *with* the seam allowances, not *against* them.

4. After you have sewn the triangles together to make the square and rectangle units for your quilt, it is very important to check the units for size and for accurate placement of the diagonal seam before sewing them into rows.

Designing by Triangle

An alternate approach to making a Blockbender quilt is to ignore light blocks and dark blocks and the number system that I have described. You may consider your strip groupings as a painter considers his palette. Cut strip-pieced triangles intu-itively, as you decide which parts of the quilt should be lighter or darker.

Mary Ellen Rees, in her quilt "Space Curves, Blocks Bend, and Away We Go," used one light strategy for the echoing open diamonds and another for the background. She made value decisions by triangle, rather than by square or rectangle unit, as there are some places where a long dark strip on one triangle meets a long light strip on its mate in the same unit.

Space Curves, Blocks Bend, and Away We Go by Mary Ellen Rees, 1994, Seattle, Washington, 75" x 99". This quilt is based on a variation of Grid E. It forced Mary Ellen to enlarge her design wall to three times its original size!

Borders for Blockbender Quilts

It is not always necessary to have a formal border on your Blockbender quilt. Sometimes the line design of the piece stands on its own. But if you want to add a border, it is important to use it to enhance the motion in the middle of the quilt or to give the design a resting place at the outer edges.

The purpose of a border on a Blockbender quilt is *not* to "hold the center in" like a frame around an oil painting.

In your efforts to "reach for the unexpected" in your border design, consider some of the following alternatives.

Asymmetrical Setting

Set your Blockbender quilt askew within the border's edges. Doreen Rennschmid used this approach in her quilt "Catch a Falling Square." She used Grid A, which has a rather predictable design, for the main body of the quilt. However, by rotating the grid within the quilt and by continuing parts of the design into the border, Doreen created a new design with this grid and its setting.

Another stunning example of this approach is Marty Kutz's quilt "The Colors of Our Skin Are God's Design" on page 75. The corners of Grid B, turned on-point, are centered at the top and bottom of the quilt. The hand-dyed fabric is not centered behind it. Since this fabric is also used in the upper triangles of this quilt, it appears that the lower triangles are "floating" over the surface. Her quilt is another example of how to use a predictable grid pattern and make it visually smashing!

Off-center Setting

Even though the edges of your pieced grid are parallel to the edges of the quilt, consider placing your quilt somewhere other than dead-center within the borders. In the illustrations at right, note that the quilt can be placed in various locations within the border. One way to achieve this is to make the border width different on each side.

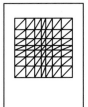

◀ **Catch a Falling Square** by Doreen Rennschmid, 1994, Sardis, British Columbia, 48" x 48". Doreen took the very predictable Grid A and made it sing a new song by setting it asymmetrically onto the border. Allowing the dark bands to escape the grid into the border area on two sides is also an important visual factor in this striking quilt.

By applying a different border width "north and south" than you do "east and west," you can create an interesting visual resting place. The border within a border on my quilt "Trail of Diamonds" on page 49 is not the same width all around. I added one row of units to the right side of Grid F as the design developed.

A variation on this theme was used by Avis Caddell in her quilt "It's a Jungle in There: A Quilt-er's Statement on Corporate Life." Avis started with Grid A and added a network of open diamonds. When she looked at the design on-point, the image of a skyscraper emerged. She added extra borders only to the sky area. In addition, Avis trimmed away some of the on-point units to create a rectangular quilt. If she had not trimmed the quilt, it would have been an irregular diamond shape.

It's a Jungle in There: A Quilter's Statement on Corporate Life, designed by Avis Caddell, pieced and quilted by Avis with Marguerite McCallion, 1994, Victoria, British Columbia, 44½" x 49". This quilt began with Grid A, but it was turned on point, and some of the grid units were eliminated to enable the skyscraper image to emerge. Appliqué elements seem to escape from the jungle prints in the "windows." Note that the illusion of the building's great height was achieved by moving from light values at the base of the building to dark values at the top, then changing abruptly to light values in the sky area.

Adding Rows

Add a row of units that continue the grid. The row could contrast with the quilt's center, not only in width but also in line design. For example, change the direction of the diagonal lines from the outside rows of the quilt to the border row as shown at right. Or, use diagonal lines in the border to echo some of the design lines found in the quilt center as shown at right.

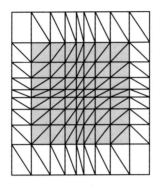

Change direction of lines in border.

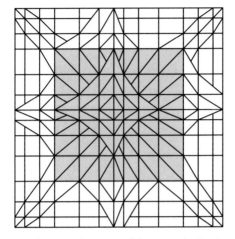

Echo direction of center quilt lines into the border.

Mary Ann Musgrove's quilt "Running with Margaret" on page 46 reflects this approach. Mary Ann began designing the border by taking two snapshots of her quilt. She trimmed away the background around the quilt in one photo and then placed it on top of the other untrimmed photo. She studied various border designs by rotating and moving the top photo around on the untrimmed photo. Sometimes, she placed it one row inside the outer edge and sometimes two rows inside. She decided to extend the fuchsia and green bands out into the border in unexpected places. Note the effectiveness of the very narrow periwinkle inner border; it emphasizes the separation between the body of the quilt and its border.

Discontinuous Border

Instead of making your border line design extend continuously around all four sides of the quilt, make it appear in specific areas but not in others.

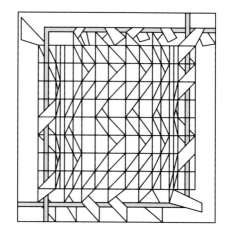

Diane Lovitt applied this design approach to her quilt "Blending the Bulging Blasted Border Blocks," which began with Grid B. Once Diane placed most of the triangles on her design wall, she folded her drawing along some of the lines to create an oval shape. Then she placed the drawing on another piece of graph paper and designed the border.

Blending the Bulging ▶ Blasted Border Blocks by Diane L. Lovitt, 1993, Pleasanton, California, 53" x 63³/₄". The irregular shape of this quilt was achieved by folding back on some of the diagonal design lines of the grid, then drawing in "straight" border lines behind the folded ones on a piece of graph paper. Diane's husband, John, was so taken by the colors in this piece, that she presented it to him for their twenty-eighth wedding anniversary!

Interrupting the Unit Sequence

Some borders are refreshing if the sequence of lines within the body of the quilt is not extended into the borders. For example, in Grid B, the units are larger in the center and become smaller as they approach the outer edges of the quilt. One border possibility for this quilt is to transition to very large units again, though not necessarily using the same-size units on all four sides of the quilt.

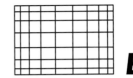

B

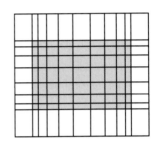

The illustrations here show other design possibilities that demonstrate the concept of interrupting the sequence or changing the scale of the units, using grids found in Appendix A.

Nancy Chong's quilt "Margaret's Window," based on Grid D, is a good example of changing the unit scale. Nancy changed the scale of the border triangles. The change in scale is accentuated within the units themselves, because she switched to subtle prints in the last row of units. In doing so, Nancy gave the quilt a quiet resting place.

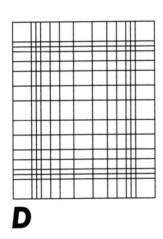

D

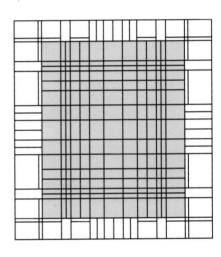

Doreen Rennschmid's pair of quilts, "Exploding Star #1" and "Exploding Star #2" on page 43, also demonstrate an effective use of this border approach. By adding very narrow borders to these quilts, Doreen put a definitive visual finish to the designs. The unit size is small in the center and grows as it approaches the outer edges of the quilt.

Another way to interrupt the unit sequence is to reverse the values, as in my quilt "Gaslamp Quarter" on page 74. I added two rows of units to Grid E and continued the sequence of rainbow-colored triangles into the borders. I reversed the value sequence of the brown triangles, however.

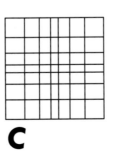

C

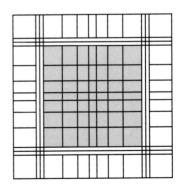

Margaret's Window by Nancy Lee Chong, 1994, Woodinville, Washington, 53" x 45". Note the subtlety of the triangles in the outermost row of units in this quilt based on Grid D. In some places, the contrast in texture between the two triangles is so low that, from a distance, the border appears to be a single fabric.

Border within a Border

On any given grid, consider creating an inner border that lies at least one row inside the outer edge. Within the inner border, use values that are quite a bit darker or lighter than the values in the adjacent units. Look at the mock-up illustrations on page 68 to see how effective this approach can be.

If strip-pieced triangles are used in most of the quilt units, use single-fabric triangles in a border within a border. You can also use a different motif to create an inner border, as in my quilt "Trail of Diamonds" on page 49.

Allowing the Design to "Escape"

In many of the Blockbender quilts, a motif approaches the edges and begs to be continued into a portion of the border. The quilt "Turn It Any Way, We Love You" on page 49, designed by Nancy Lee Chong and Elizabeth Hendricks, is just such a quilt. Note how the heart shapes continue into, but do not extend completely across, the checkerboard border.

Julie Tollefson's quilt "Up and Down Blockbender Hearts II" is another example of how the theme of the quilt escaped into the border. Julie not only completed the two heart motifs in

Up and Down Blockbender Hearts II by Julie Tollefson, 1994, Camano Island, Washington, 60" x 62". Machine quilted by Patsi Hanseth, Mount Vernon, Washington. This quilt is based on Grid C and uses the "spotlight in the center" light strategy. It could be subtitled "Yin and Yang Hearts." Note how quickly the values move from light to dark.

▼

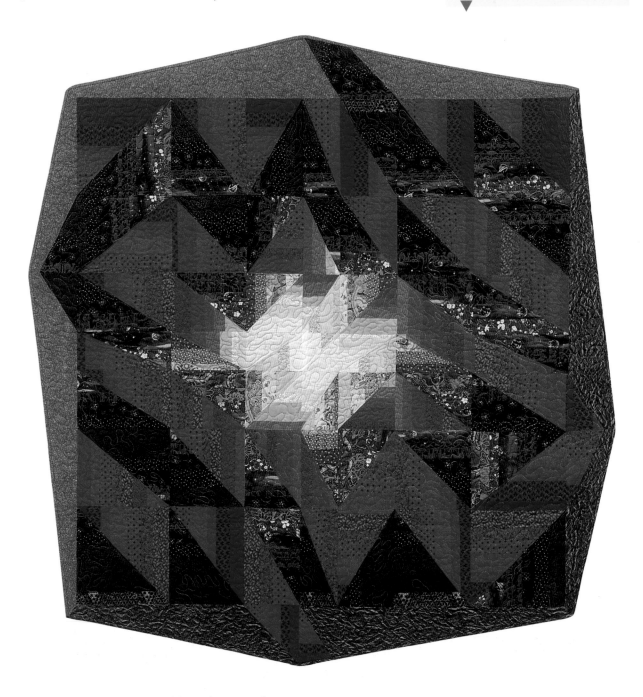

the side borders, she allowed a band of color to pierce the north and south borders.

Notice, too, that the edges of the quilt need not be parallel to the edges of the design grid. The possibilities for this type of border design are limited only by your ability to design a way to hang your quilt!

Using Your Leftovers

Add a wide border that includes your leftover triangles. Piece or appliqué them in place to create the illusion that the triangles have been blown away from the quilt's center into the border area. The border on my quilt "Carousel" on page 92 demonstrates this approach.

You will need to decide whether to sprinkle the triangles in an organized pattern within the border, scatter them in certain areas, or concentrate them in one or two areas. Depending on the design in the middle of your quilt, consider piecing or appliquéing leftover triangles in a formal arrangement. Think about appliquéing some of the triangles so that they camouflage the lines where the body of the quilt meets the border.

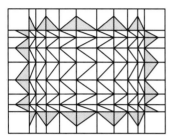

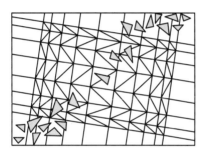

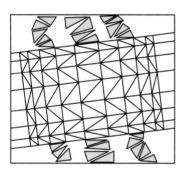

Adding Random Strip Piecing

Make strip-pieced fabric using all the colors and values that appear in the center of the quilt. Use the pieced fabric in your border. Orient the strips so that they are perpendicular, parallel, or placed at an angle to the edges of the quilt. Remember, the border does not need to be the same width on all four sides. Look at the borders on my quilt "Beacon Clearing" on page 70 and Kerry Hoffman's "Venetian Ribbons" on page 61.

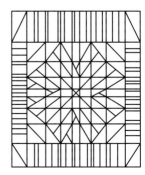

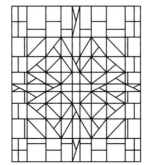

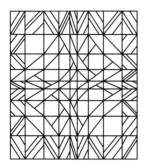

Flights of Fancy

By now, you realize the numerous visual effects that are possible when you use the Blockbender grids. Still more variations occur when you apply a broad range of colors and values to the design and when you use either single-fabric or strip-pieced triangles (or both) within the units.

The range of design possibilities becomes even more vast when you combine multiple grids, rotate segments of grids, cut grids into segments, or create your own grids.

Adding or Subtracting Rows

The changes you make in the grid can be minor, such as adding or subtracting a row of units. Using Grid E as an example, notice that the open diamond on the right edge of the quilt is incomplete in the illustration at top right. But, by adding a single vertical row of units to the middle of the grid, the entire diamond appears in the design.

Add rows of units in order to create enough background area to emphasize the central design. Conversely, you may wish to reduce a grid by one or more rows or columns of units to accommodate a particular design. You may decide to wait to amend your original design until after you have placed most of the triangles on your design wall.

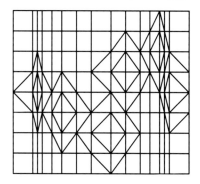

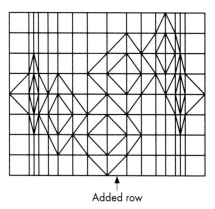

Added row

Using Multiple Grids Together

To experiment with this technique, make photocopies of grids that have your favorite line designs on them. Trim around them so that you can place them edge to edge. Make multiple photocopies of your new grid and use colored pencils to play with color combinations. Challenge yourself to place color so differently from one quilt plan to another that no one will realize that you have used the same line design!

Julie Tollefson's quilt "Up and Down Blockbender Hearts I" on page 45 is an example of two Grid B designs joined together.

The quilt plan below started with all lines drawn in one direction on Grid C. Two photocopies of this "ordinary" Grid C were taped together edge to edge, and a series of half diagonals were drawn across the grid. The mock-ups on page 116 show how different this simple line design looks when fabric is applied.

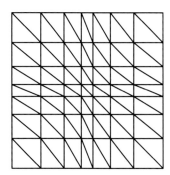

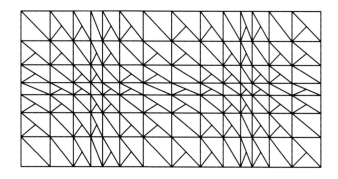

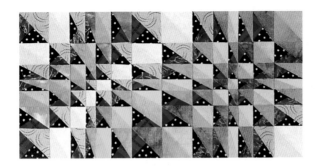 

Take multiple snapshots of a Blockbender quilt in progress, standing at the same distance from your design wall. Cut the snapshots apart or trim the snapshots, then place multiple parts edge to edge as shown. You will probably discover new possibilities for an otherwise predictable quilt.

Note that when you design Blockbender quilts using multiple photographs, you need to carefully consider the finished size of the quilt. For example, the body of the original quilt measures 60" x 64". The next version measures 120" x 64". The last version measures 128" x 60". To create a reasonably sized quilt using this design method, consider working with three-quarter-size or half-size templates.

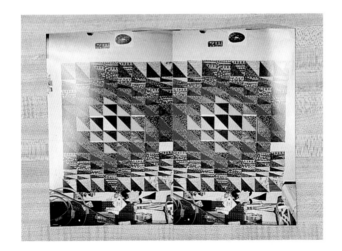

Rotating Grids

Try the following exercises to see the design potential of rotating multiple grids. Make at least four photocopies of the grids below. Each is a portion of Grid A. Draw a different line design in each of the eight grids. Next, make four photocopies of each of your favorite line designs.

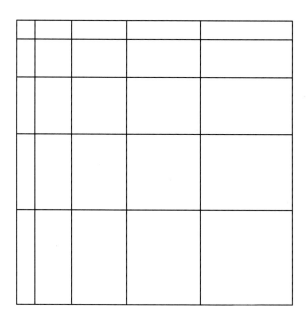 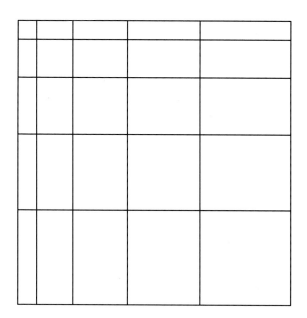

Trim away the excess paper around your four photocopies of one line design. Label the corners of each of them identically as shown. "A" should be in the smallest unit, and "C" should be in the largest one. Be sure to letter the drawing in clockwise fashion.

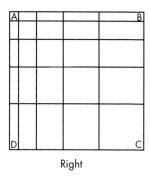
Right

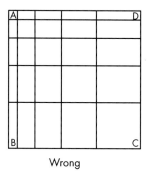
Wrong

In the first rotation, place the photocopies edge to edge with all "A's" in the upper left-hand corner.

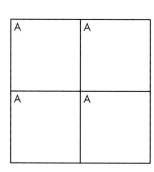

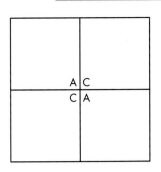

Next, place 2 A's and 2 C's so they meet at the center.

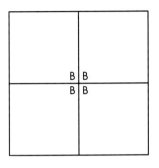
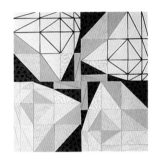

Next, place all B's to the center. All the grid lines will not match up, but this sometimes leads to very interesting design possibilities. A pinwheel design appears in the center where the four B corners come together.

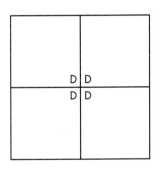

By placing all D's to the center, another pinwheel appears—this one spins in the opposite direction! Some line designs look better with B's to the center, some with D's to the center, so be sure to try both.

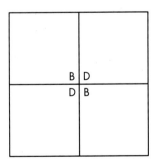
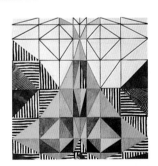

Place 2 B's and 2 D's to the center, corner to corner. Some grid and line designs yield an hourglass motif in this arrangement.

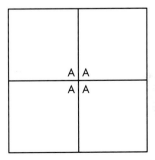

When you arrange all A's to the center, the most intense area of design is placed in the center of the quilt. Nancy Lee Chong used this rotation in her quilt "Silent Running."

Silent Running by Nancy Lee Chong, 1994, Woodinville, Washington, 86" x 86". This quilt was the result of a challenge between Nancy and her sister Janice Baehr. They were to use a run of fabrics from blues to greens to yellows, all colors which were beyond Nancy's "comfort range." Nancy made four quilts based on Grid A and photographed multiple rotations of the four units, finally settling on the rotation you see here.

The last rotation—placing all C's to the center—uses the opposite strategy. It brings the most open parts of your four grids to the center, which can make your quilt look as if it is laid over a dome. Since the most intense design area is moved to the outer edges of this arrangement, a borderlike design is formed.

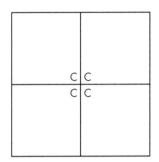 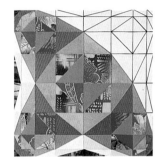 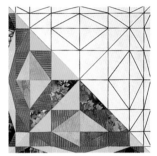

Go back to the designs you developed on the photocopies of the grids at the top of page 117. Use them to play with the rotations we just explored. Once you have seen the effects that the rotations produce, consider combining more than one block design in the same rotations as shown in the examples below.

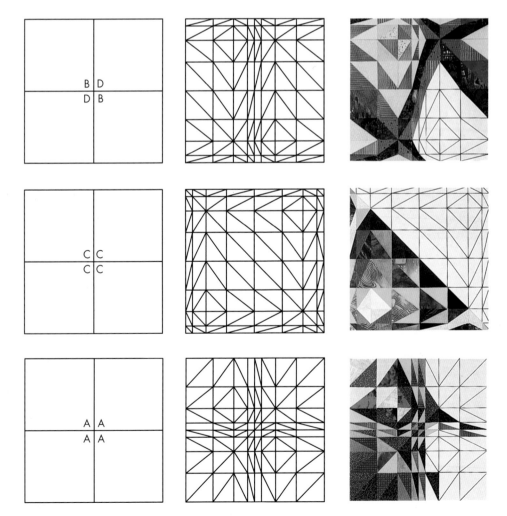

Cutting Grids into Segments

You can create other possibilities by cutting the grids into segments and reassembling them. They don't even have to be oriented the same as they appear in the original drawing.

Again, experiment with line drawings or with photographs. Take any grid and cut it apart along two or more parallel grid lines. Rejoin the segments to form a quilt, but turn every other segment upside down.

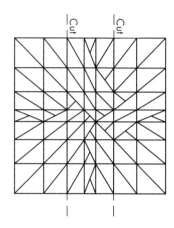
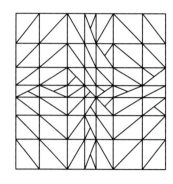

In another variation, use sashing strips of various widths to separate segments.

Try joining segments with sashing strips that are not parallel.

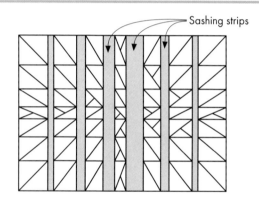

Cut the grid apart on perpendicular grid lines and then experiment with vertical and horizontal sashing strips. Consider making some sashing strips parallel to each other and then some that are not parallel.

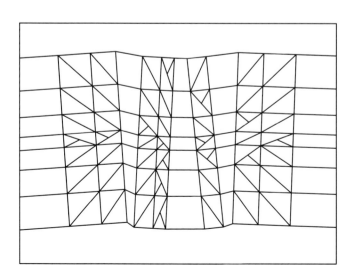
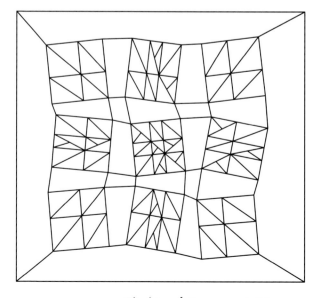

Breaking Free

By employing more than one of the options presented, imagine the stunning quilts that are possible. For example, Valerie Chapla used the "all A's to the center" rotation of Grid A but then used only a portion of the resulting design in her quilt "Space #2: To Boldly Go . . ."

Avis Caddell took "combining grids" to new heights with her quilt "Up, Up, and Away." This quilt expresses how working with the Blockbender design system has, for Avis, become an "uplifting release from those oh-so traditional roots." The balloon portion of this quilt is actually a separate quilt superimposed on the base quilt. Though the blue base quilt has a very traditional feel to it, it is created from four A grids, in an "all A's to the center" rotation. The white area where the balloon is bursting forth is actual layers of exposed quilt batting!

Flo Peel used a grid and a half in her quilt "Prairie Sunset." Note that the complete grid, a variation of Grid C, is in the upper right corner of the quilt; half versions of the same grid are located to the left and below the whole grid. The lower left corner is yet another portion of the same grid.

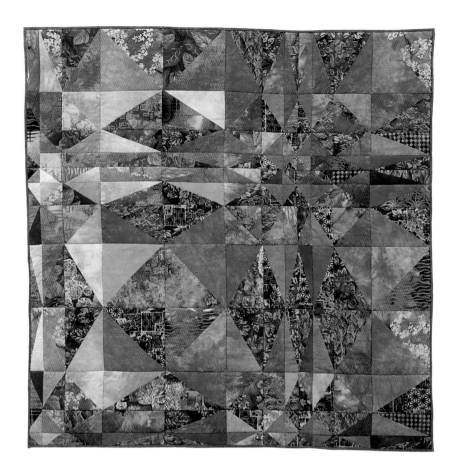

Space #2: To Boldly Go . . . by Valerie Sauban Chapla, 1993, Pleasant Hill, California, 52" x 44". This quilt was inspired by the movie "Star Trek" and is a good example of pushing your limits in moving color and light across a pieced surface. This quilt is a section of a design created by putting four Grid A's together, edge to edge.

Prairie Sunset by Flo Peel, 1994, Bowen Island, British Columbia, 50" x 50". The combination of hand-dyed and commercially printed fabrics makes this piece hauntingly beautiful. Note the subtle use of peaches and reds, which resemble dappled light emanating from a source off the upper left corner of the quilt.

Up, Up, and Away by Avis Caddell, 1994, Victoria, British Columbia, 56" x 56". The hot air balloon is a symbol for contemporary quiltmaking, breaking free from its ties to traditional work and showing new "true colors." Avis writes that this quilt is also a personal statement about her evolution as an artist, "the untethering of ideas and the heartfelt knowledge that the sky is the limit."

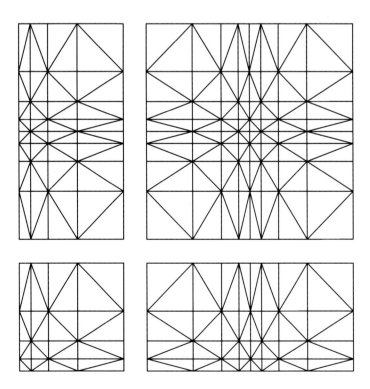

Dale MacEwan is a master at diffusing the edges of harsh grids and creating subtleties of value that bring a special soft light to her pieces. In "Japanese Mountains," note the simplicity of the line design in the grid Dale designed herself. Most of the diagonal design lines are in one direction only, but by using thirteen lines drawn in the opposite direction, she created the illusion of mountaintops.

In her quilt "Dialogue with the Trees," Dale made the most of the diagonal lines to form tree branches and used the values to create the illusion that we are looking into a thick grove of trees, suffused with light.

Elizabeth Hendricks created her own grid for "Woman in a Box." Note how she subdivided the grid further to allow more detailed shadowing of the figure.

◀ **Japanese Mountains** by Dale MacEwan, 1992, Richmond, British Columbia, 58" x 44" (collection of Patrick and Grethe Floyd, New Westminster, British Columbia). Working in the three colors of red, purple, and blue, Dale created the illusion of mountains in the sky, with a connection to the earth camouflaged by mists and banks of fog. Note how simple the line design of this quilt is, yet how elegant the final result.

Dialogue with the Trees ▶ by Dale MacEwan, 1994, Richmond, British Columbia, 54" x 62". Dale used more than sixty different fabrics and created her own grid for this piece; the grid was altered as needed where she wanted the tree branches to bend. Since Dale felt a "sense of loss when this quilt was completed," she now looks forward to using this format for a series of tree quilts.

Woman in a Box by Elizabeth ▶ Hendricks, 1994, Seattle, Washington, 72" x 80". This powerful quilt was designed and made during the time the artist was dealing with a cancer diagnosis (which was later cleared). There is much symbolism in the colors chosen: some represent fear, others depict life forces pushing out toward similar forces outside the figure—with too tenuous a connection between them. The quilting design also lends power to the quilt: skeletal patterns, representing disease, which reduces the body to its fundamental structure; lizards quilted all over the body, symbolizing both the fear crawling down the figure's back and a connection with all life. This quilt won Best of Show at the Association of Pacific Northwest Quilters Show in Seattle, Washington in July 1994.

Betty Parks takes the prize for complexity of design with her quilt "Gram's Crock, Mom's Table, My Flowers"; her background as an oil painter and avid gardener is evident in this piece. Note how strongly the Blockbender grid supports this piece. But more important, note the liberties Betty took with the strategies presented in this book. As you follow the edges of the flowers, notice how the strip piecing in any given triangle involves both the figure and the background. So, to the many possibilities resulting from grid lines and design lines, Betty added yet another alternative: new lines created by "breaks" in the strip piecing of any given triangle! You may find that your biggest challenge in working with the Blockbender grids is to stop yourself from playing too long with the line designs and the grids and *get to the fabric and make a quilt!*

▲

Gram's Crock, Mom's Table, My Flowers by Betty Parks, 1994, Snohomish, Washington, 63" x 73". Betty comes to quiltmaking from a painting background, and the crock was a signature motif in her paintings. As she let this quilt grow and "take on a life of its own," she found herself remembering her Grandmother stuffing fresh flowers into crocks at her mother's yellow-green kitchen table, hence the name of the quilt.

Detail of Gram's Crock, Mom's Table, My Flowers by Betty Parks. ▶

Quilting Designs for Blockbender Quilts

Common design elements in Blockbender quilts are the lines that change angles and appear to flow across the surface. This fluidity can be enhanced by the quilting design. The quilting lines are more effective when they meander across the blocks rather than staying within block boundaries.

Further, significant amounts of curved line quilting will surely enhance many of the designs derived through the Blockbender design process.

A number of approaches are suggested by the quilts in this book. Use them as initial nuggets of ideas, not as a complete guide to quilting-line possibilities.

If you wish to highlight an enclosed motif (like hearts or interlocking diamonds), use dense quilting in the background areas. Stipple quilting or close parallel-line quilting that echoes the motif may work well and make the motif "pop out" of the quilt surface.

Another effective method is to make the quilting lines go in directions that are opposite of the design lines. If the pieced design radiates, make quilting lines radiate through concentric quilted circles. When the pieced design forms a concave motif, surround it with quilted lines that evoke sheltering convex forms. For pieced designs that meander from one corner of the quilt to the other, stitch a quilting pattern with a repeating rectangular motif that parallels the edge of the quilt.

It pays to take your time deciding on a quilting design; snapshots are very useful in this process. Place a snapshot of your quilt (in which the image of the quilt is as large as possible) under a piece of tracing paper or a plastic report cover. Draw quilting designs on the tracing paper or plastic, using a pencil or a fine felt-tip pen.

If you would like to work on a larger piece of paper, make an enlarged photocopy of your grid (with the design lines in place). Shade it very lightly with colored pencils. Place tracing paper over it and, with meandering pencil lines, begin experimenting with quilt designs. Place this line design on your design wall and stand away from it to study it.

Blockbender quilts are also very good candidates for machine quilting because they have so many seams, especially where the triangles are strip-pieced.

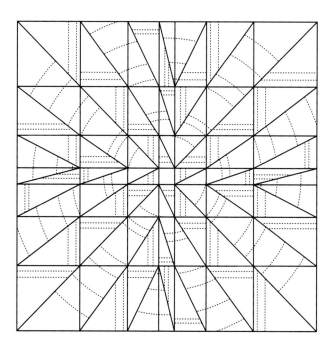

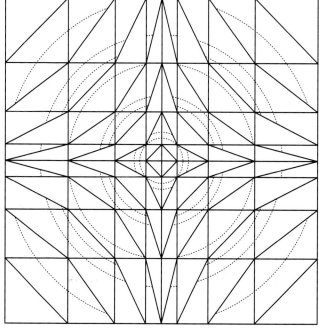

Afterword

Over the years, I have been inspired by words on many different topics—words of wisdom that affect my creative life and my life as a teacher. The sources of these words are varied, from notes tacked to kitchen cupboard doors in friends' homes, to numerous books and magazines. Other favorite sources are biographies of artists and others I admire.

One of the quotations I stumbled on is attributed to General Norman Schwartzkoff. It characterizes the essentials of good teaching, which can take place in a classroom, during a guild meeting, a satellite group gathering, or through the pages of a book. He said, "A good teacher does not strive to explain his vision—he invites you to stand beside him and see for yourself."

For me, the thrill of teaching quiltmaking is dropping a new idea into the pond and watching the students carry it where they may. I would only add, dear reader, that, as you create your own Blockbender quilts through the pages of this book, you not only *see* for yourself, but very much *enjoy the view.*

To obtain information on lectures, workshops, and other books by the author, write to Margaret at the following address:

That Patchwork Place
PO Box 118
Bothell, Washington
98041-0118

Meet the Author

Margaret J. Miller is a studio quiltmaker who travels widely giving lectures and workshops on color and design, encouraging students to "reach for the unexpected" in contemporary quiltmaking. Her full teaching schedule has taken her throughout the United States, as well as to Australia, Denmark, New Zealand, and South Africa. Margaret is known for her enthusiastic, humorous presentations in which she sincerely encourages quiltmakers of all skill levels and experience.

Though she has done various forms of needlework throughout her life, Margaret began to quilt and appliqué in 1978. At that time, she was on the faculty of the home economics department at California Polytechnic State University, San Luis Obispo, teaching creative textiles. After moving to San Diego, Margaret started "Tangle-thread Junction," a pattern business featuring appliqué and stained-glass appliqué designs. In 1982 she sold her business to become a full-time quiltmaker.

In addition to *Blockbender Quilts*, she is the author of *Blockbuster Quilts* (1991) and *Strips That Sizzle* (1992), both published by That Patchwork Place. In addition, her chapter "Bloomin' Quilt Grids" appears in the book *Quilt with the Best* (Oxmoor House, 1992). She also wrote the introduction to the Quilt San Diego catalog, *Visions: The Art of the Quilt* (C & T Publishing, 1992).

Margaret lives near Seattle, Washington, with her husband and their two "almost launched" sons to whom this book is lovingly dedicated. She is frequently accompanied in her studio (which was once the formal living and dining rooms) by two cats and a boxer puppy named Cal, who keeps the whole household laughing.

Appendix A: Grids, Blockbender Grids, and Sample Work Sheets

Use photocopies of this page for design exercises, which begin on page 14.

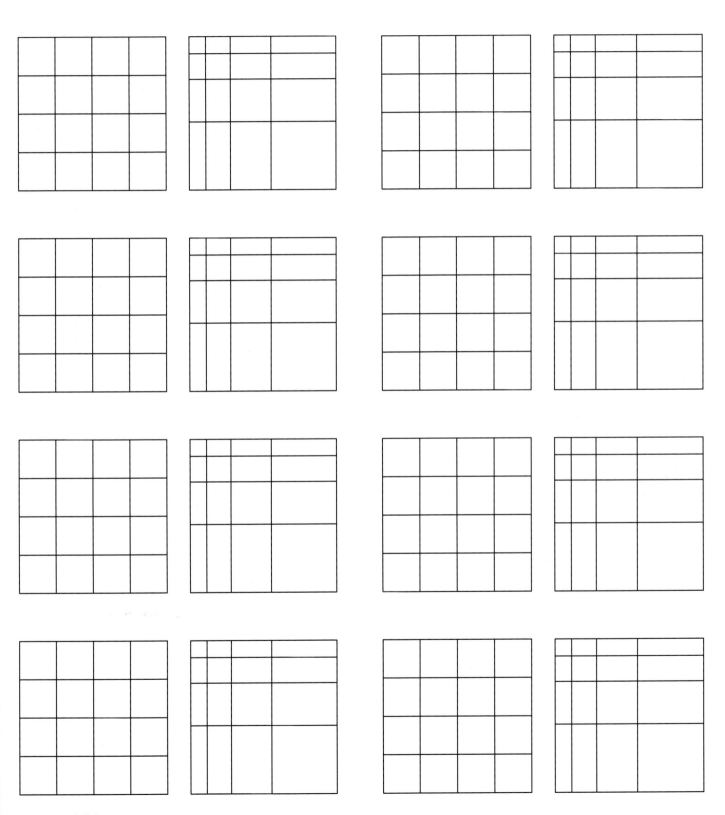

Photocopies of pages 131–39 may be made for your use only. The traditional grids have the same number of units as the Blockbender grids on the same page. Use the traditional grid to "try out" a line design before working with the Blockbender grid.

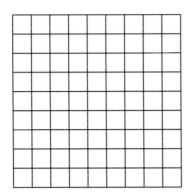

Grid A

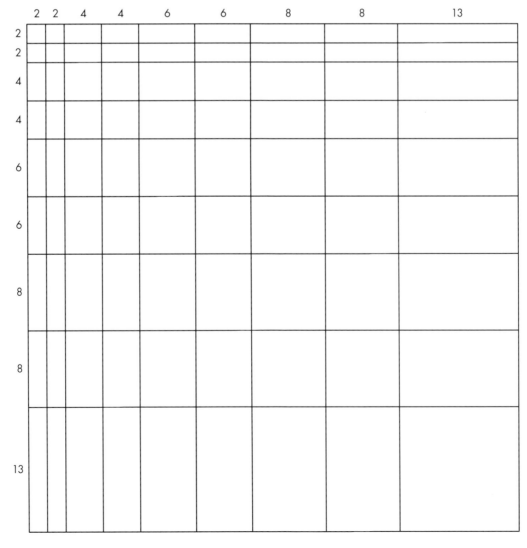

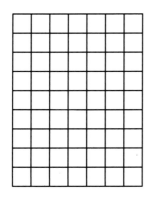

Grid B

	4	6	8	10	8	6	4
4							
6							
8							
10							
12							
10							
8							
6							
4							

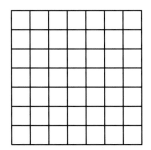

Grid C

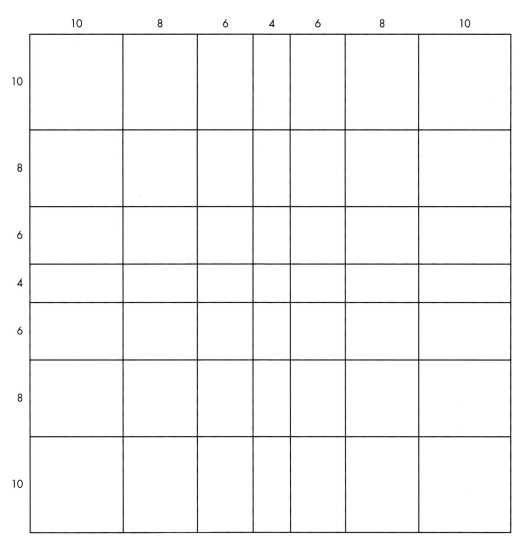

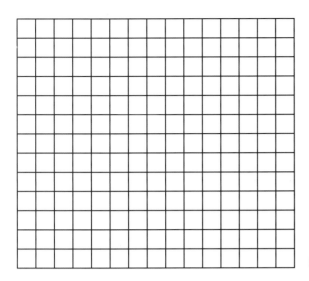

Grid D

	8	2	2	4	4	6	6	8	6	6	4	4	2	2	8
8															
2															
2															
4															
4															
6															
8															
6															
4															
4															
2															
2															
8															

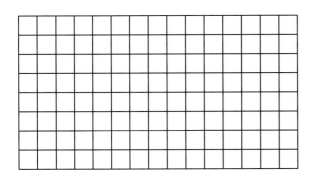

Grid E

	8	2	2	4	4	6	6	8	6	6	4	4	2	2	8
8															
8															
8															
8															
8															
8															
8															
8															

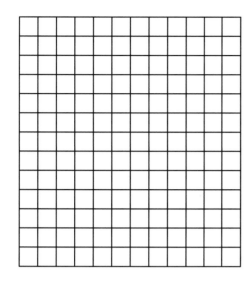

Grid F

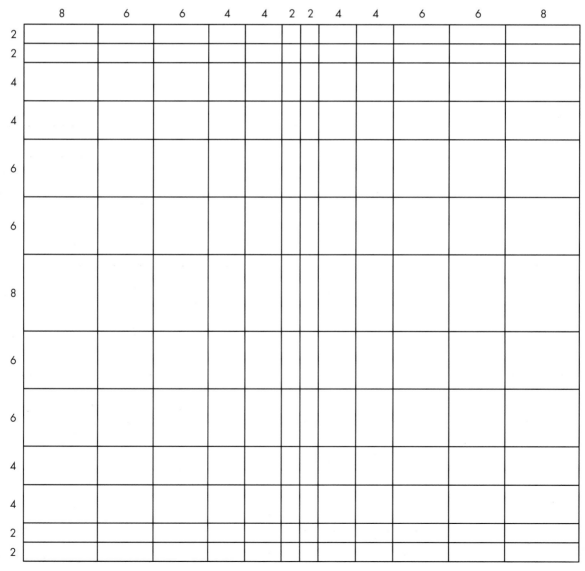

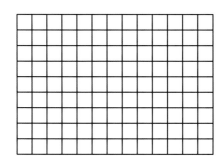

Grid G

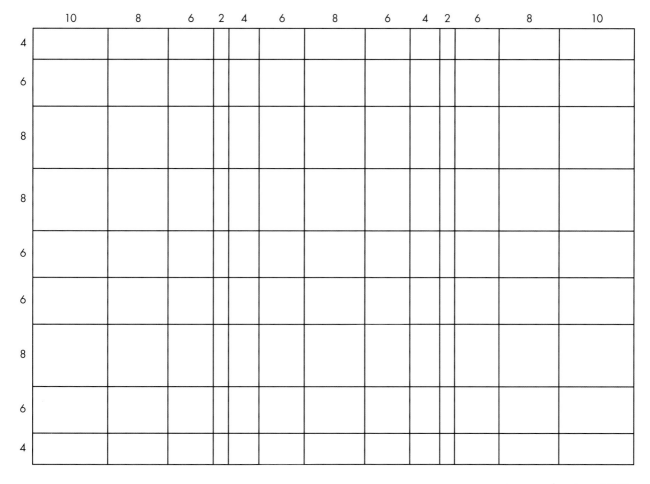

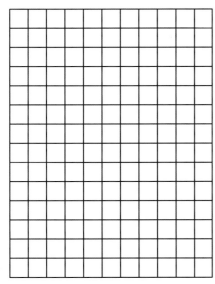

Grid H

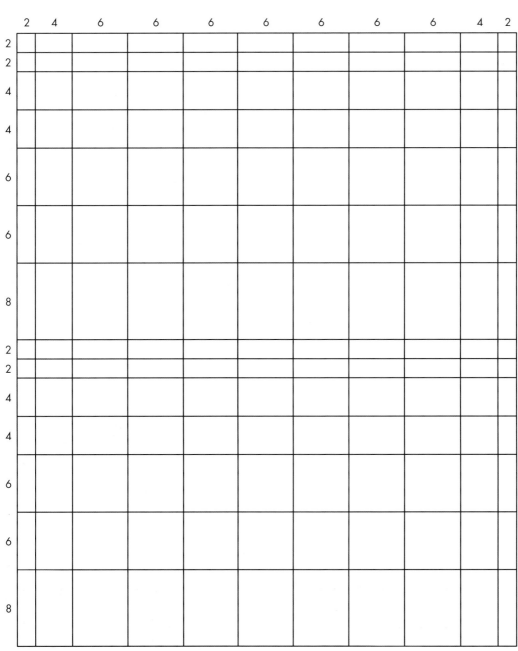

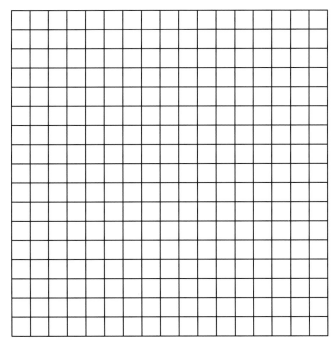

Grid I

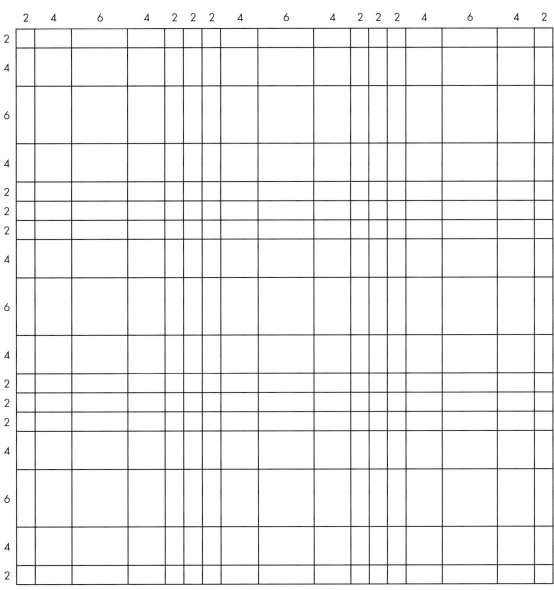

Appendix B: *Multiple Color Families*

Blockbender quilts, especially those based on strip-pieced triangles, lend themselves to using multiple color families or a progression from one color family to another. Choosing multiple color families and using multiple values in those color families is not as difficult as inexperienced quiltmakers might think.

The following process for selecting harmonious colors was developed by Johannes Itten and is one every art student learns early in his or her color education. An abbreviated version of this color theory is presented here; explore this area further by studying basic books on color theory and art principles.

To begin, trace the four templates on page 142 onto paper or plastic and cut them out so they can be superimposed on the color wheel on page 142.

When you place either of the triangles onto the color wheel, the three color categories in which the points of the triangle fall are harmonious. Fabrics chosen from these categories would

go well together in a quilt. Rotate the triangles around the color wheel to choose a number of harmonious triads. The equilateral triangle (template 1) can form four different color groupings as shown below.

The isosceles triangle (template 2), however, can be rotated to select twelve different harmonious color triads.

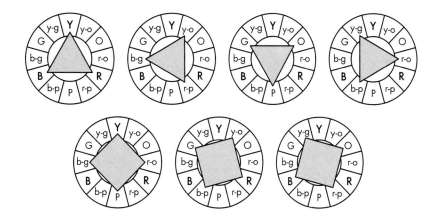

The square and rectangular templates (templates 3 and 4) can be used in the same manner as the triangles to select harmonious pairs of complementary colors, or tetrads. Notice that the square can be used to select three different four-color groupings in rotation around the color wheel, while the rectangle can be rotated to six different positions.

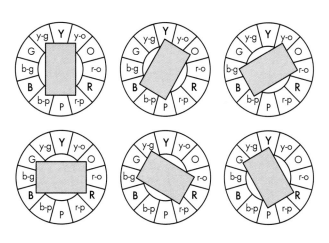

Remember that these are ways to choose the color families only. You still need to work with a wide range of values within the color families you select. It would be an interesting experiment for you to pull fabrics from your collection to represent each of these triads and tetrads. Given your current fabric collection, would you be able to work with many of these three- and four-color groupings? If you want to force yourself out of your "comfort zone" of using the same colors over and over again, use this system of selecting color families the next time you shop for fabric.

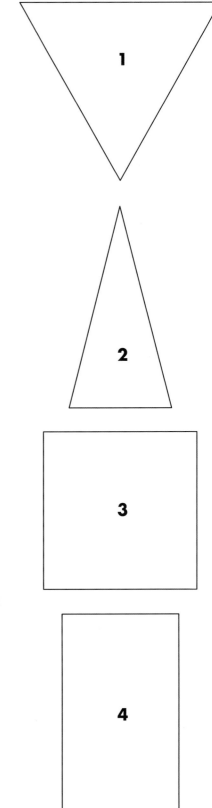

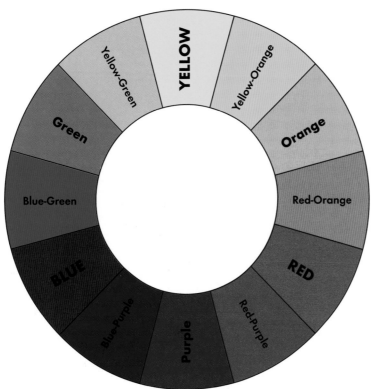

Sources

Graph Paper

The cross-section graph paper (8 squares per inch) that I recommend is hard to find in some areas of the country. If you cannot find pads of it in your local art-supply store, office-products store, or college bookstore, call the companies listed below and ask them where you can find this graph paper in your area.

MacPherson's

(Northern California; source for Morilla brand)

1-800-289-9800

Bienfang

(Oregon; source for 8½" x 11", 11" x 17", and 17" x 22" pads)

1-800-547-1544

Hand-Dyed Fabric

Throughout this book are quilts that include hand-dyed fabric. Here are sources for that wonderful stuff!

ARTFABRIK

c/o Melody Johnson
and Laura Wasilowski
664 W. Main St.
Cary, IL 60013
(708) 639-5966

Country Hill Press

(Home of Sueded Cottons and other Delights)
c/o Debra Thomas
PO Box 1016
Keller, TX 76248
(817) 431-6029

DYEnamic Fabrics and Designs

c/o Libit Woodington
PO Box 765
Columbia, SC 29202
(803) 771-6524

Kaleidoscope Designs

c/o Florence E. Peel
RR #1, Box Y-13
Bowen Island,
British Columbia
V0N 1G0 Canada

Bibliography

Itten, Johannes. *The Elements of Color.* Edited by Faber Birren. New York: Van Nostrand Reinhold, 1970.

Miller, Margaret J. *Blockbuster Quilts.* Bothell, Wash.: That Patchwork Place, Inc., 1991.

Miller, Margaret J. *Strips That Sizzle.* Bothell, Wash.: That Patchwork Place, Inc., 1992.

For the quilts of Jan Myers-Newbury, see:

Hagood, Carol Cook, ed. *Quilt with the Best.* Birmingham, Ala.: Oxmoor House, Inc., 1992, pp. 140–59.

That Patchwork Place Publications and Products